BIGGER THAN A BREADBOX

Books by Steve Allen

BIGGER THAN A BREADBOX

STEVE ALLEN

WITH A COMMENTARY BY
LEONARD FEATHER

MR. ALLEN'S CARTOON IDEAS
ILLUSTRATED BY
ROWLAND B. WILSON

DOUBLEDAY & COMPANY, INC.   GARDEN CITY, NEW YORK
1967

Grateful acknowledgment is made to the following:

CBS Radio and Abe Burrows, for permission to use an interview from Steve Allen's CBS Radio program of August 13, 1952.

Down Beat, for permission to use a record review by George Hoefer, from the October 29, 1959, issue of *Down Beat;* and two poems by Steve Allen, "Jazz Mass at St. Paul's" (May 28, 1959), and "Death of the Blues."

Leland Hayward Productions, Inc., for permission to use "The True Blue American" by Steve Allen with Buck Henry, which appeared, in slightly altered form, on *That Was the Week That Was.*

Holt, Rinehart and Winston, Inc., for permission to use "The End of the World" and "There, but for the Grace of God, Goes Harry Truman," from *Mark It and Strike It* by Steve Allen. Copyright © 1960 by Jayne Meadows Allen, Jules L. Green, and Irving Cohen. Reprinted by permission.

National Broadcasting Company, Inc., for permission to use material from the WNBC-TV *Tonight Show* starring Steve Allen.

Redbook Magazine, for permission to use "The Secret I Can No Longer Live With" by Steve Allen. Reprinted from *Redbook Magazine.* Copyright © 1960 by McCall Corporation.

Simon & Schuster, Inc., for permission to use "Three Mixed-up Little Pigs" from *Bop Fables* by Steve Allen, copyright © 1955 by Steve Allen; and for permission to quote from *The Funny Men* by Steve Allen, copyright © 1956 by Steve Allen. Reprinted by permission.

The Straus Broadcasting Group, Inc., Jim Moran, and Bob Carroll, for permission to use interviews from the WMCA *The Barry Gray Show.*

World Journal Tribune, Inc., for permission to quote from a column by John Crosby from the former New York *Herald Tribune.*

CONTENTS

BIGGER THAN A BREADBOX

Perhaps a brief explanation of the title of this book is warranted, for the benefit of those too young to remember the early days of "What's My Line?"

On that long-lived program, the panelists, one of whom was Steve Allen (regularly from 1951–53, and intermittently thereafter until the program's demise), tried to determine the occupation of a guest. This often involved guessing at the nature of a product with which the guest might be identified and, to that end, finding out the size of the product. Allen's commonest question along this interrogative route, heard so often that it became a running gag, was "Is it bigger than a breadbox?"

There is, of course, nothing inherently comic about a breadbox. Yet the question, after it had been used regularly for a while, came to generate an aura of amusement because it was a predictable verbal gambit, symbolic of the spirit of good humor that characterized the show.

If only for this reason, the book's title is appropriate: a breadbox or almost anything else, tangible or intangible, can give rise to an atmosphere of risibility under the right conditions, particularly when the speaker or writer has the unique wit of a Steve Allen. In the final analysis, the dimensions of humor are greater than those of comedy—bigger than a breadbox, larger than laughter, vaster than life.

COMEDY, HUMOR, AND ALLEN

by Leonard Feather

"Sports fans," Steve Allen once said, "I have a final score for you on that big game between Harvard and William and Mary. Final score: Harvard 14, William 12, Mary 6."

A doctor whom Allen was interviewing on the air said to him, "The only two really instinctive fears in man are the fear of loud noises and the fear of falling. What are *you* afraid of?"

"I have a great fear," Allen admitted, "of making a loud noise while falling."

At a gathering at the Herbert Bayard Swope apartment one evening the subject of motion picture production came up.

"Let's see," somebody said, "who was it who made *Helen of Troy?*"

"Fellow named Paris," was Steve's suggestion.

On "Long John" Nebel's radio show, New York newsman John Wingate said to Steve, "Ratings are difficult but they're part of TV reality. How do you beat them?"

"With a stick," Allen answered.

Milt Hoffman, producer of one of Allen's TV programs, said, "Some teen-age punks were causing trouble outside our theater the other night. The police came along and booked them."

"Yes," Steve said, "but they booked them into the Playboy Club."

Hearing a certain political figure referred to as "a man of conviction," Allen said, "Yes, for larceny, forgery, assault and battery . . ."

Somebody once asked Allen, "Do you think it is proper for an unmarried girl to sleep with a man?"

"By no means," he said. "She should stay awake all night. You don't know *what* might happen while you're asleep."

New York disc jockey Joe Franklin once said to Steve, "I don't want to put words in your mouth."

"I don't know of a better place," was the humorist's answer.

On his TV program a guest—purporting to analyze Allen's character by reading his palm—said, "One good thing about you is that you're loyal to a fault."

"You're right," Steve said. "I've got a great many faults and I'm loyal to every one of them."

A mind playful enough to spontaneously create humor such as this might not seem easily given to pessimism, but in an article written several years ago for *Atlantic Monthly*, Steve Allen held up a telescope to the past as well as a periscope to the future of American comedy. His conclusions were gloomy. He found the low common denominator of popular taste swinging away from the humorist and comedian toward Westerns and quiz shows. "The comedians who continue to function despite the trend," he wrote, "are subject to increasingly heavy at-

tacks from critics, audiences, rating services, and from
the vaguely defined spirit of the times."

These comments were written in 1957. In today's light
it would appear that Allen was viewing with unnecessary
alarm a scene subject to constant change, one in which
he may have tended to equate alteration with disinte-
gration.

His statement that "the hearty halcyon days of Charlie
Chaplin, Harold Lloyd, Laurel and Hardy, Joe E.
Brown, Fatty Arbuckle, Charlie Chase, W. C. Fields,
Harry Langdon, Edgar Kennedy, Jack Oakie, the Marx
Brothers, and Mack Sennett's assorted clowns are clearly
not to be duplicated," reads today like a report that because we now have no Beethovens, Bachs, or Gershwins,
music is dead; or because Quentin Reynolds and Ed-
ward R. Murrow are gone, the era of great reporting is
irretrievably lost.

The retrospective regret for past glories is invariably
tinged with nostalgia, sometimes to the point where there
is confusion between intrinsic merit and highly subjective
personal associations. If a Charlie Chase or a Harry
Langdon came along today, just how funny would he
seem? And how much of an impact could he make on
the far more sophisticated comedy audience of this nuclear age?

The fact is that humor is shaped by the cross winds of
time. Even comedy that seems not to be inherently topi-
cal nevertheless may lose its freshness and impact simply
because of the altered conditioning of the audience exposed to it. Some of the silent movies and early talking-
pictures made thirty or forty years ago by the artists on
Allen's list are still inherently funny in part, but certain

sequences and premises have dated to the point where we can scarcely understand let alone laugh at them. This is true more of verbal than of visual comedy, yet both forms have suffered from the process that overtakes many of the popular arts: continuous imitation has ruined the impact of the original, and continuous sharpening of our responses has rendered feeble and naïve what once seemed keenly witty.

The attrition of the years may have debilitated or destroyed some of the comedy of yesteryear, but it has not yet put all the pioneer comedians on the sidelines. Allen's pessimistic survey implied that by the mid-1960s Jack Benny, Groucho Marx, Jimmy Durante, and Burns and Allen would probably no longer be active. We have lost Gracie Allen, but the others remain at this writing, late 1966, though none are presented regularly on TV. Allen himself now agrees that only as regards television was his pessimism justified.

Comedy today, though rarely on TV, is more than ever a mirror of the period in history that shapes it. In the mid-1960s, in a world in which awareness of the frightening realities around us perhaps weakens the appeal of the more casual levities, there has emerged a new brand of comedian who assumes more and more a certain knowledge and sophistication on the part of his audience. As a consequence, iconoclasm, the evolution of sexual taboos, and the open discussion of racial topics once considered beyond the comic pale are providing new territories on which new breeds of funny men tread with assurance.

Compensatory factors have arisen that have all but eliminated the necessity to weep over the loss of the definitive comedy personalities of the 1920s and thirties.

Changes in the sociopsychological environment have brought the emergence, for example, of a new school of Negro comedians. Most of them are as far removed from Stepin Fetchit and Manton Moreland as *Ranger IV* is from the *Spirit of St. Louis*. Dick Gregory's a priori assumptions—that the audience is with him, can laugh with him against Governor Wallace, can sympathize with his deep involvement in the civil rights movement—would have been inconceivable during the McCarthy era. This is true even of the nonracial comedy of a Bill Cosby, which makes a second assumption: you can accept me as an articulate man dressed in normal clothes and speaking without a southern drawl; you and I can laugh together at a common object of ridicule that has no relationship to race.

America's sense of humor, in fact (the term automatically comprises a *taste* for humor and a *sense* of comedy), has been broadening steadily. Eight years after his negative analysis was printed, Steve Allen sounded a more optimistic note; he insisted that the comedy of today is wonderfully fresh and vigorous.

Possibly the most reassuring proof that the audience for comedy is expanding in breadth and depth is the recent history of Allen himself.

If it were necessary, in inspecting the humor of the mid-twentieth century, to confine all one's examination to a single man, Steve Allen certainly would provide the perfect synthesis. On one program or another, in one medium or another, at one point or another in his twenty-year career as a comedian, he has been involved with the dissemination and interpretation of almost every important branch of humor and comedy. (As he has pointed out, the word *comedy* suggests the idea of performance, while the word *humor* suggests creative thinking and the written word; but there is a considerable area of overlap.)

There have been observed in the humor and comedy of Steve Allen elements of the ad-lib effrontery of Groucho Marx, the sardonic ellipsis of Henry Morgan, the quiet understatement of Dave Garroway, the neighborliness of Arthur Godfrey, the irony and hipness of Dick Gregory, the stand-up glibness of Bob Hope, the physical comedy of Red Skelton, the exaggeration of Sid Caesar, and the prose wit of the late Robert Benchley. It is not simply that he is a complete eclectic, though his book *The Funny Men* made it clear that he had analyzed with extraordinary sensitivity the techniques of many of his contemporaries; it is rather that Allen himself, as a comedian, intrinsically possesses some of the characteristics of all these men while still maintaining his own originality.

In several respects, however, he differs from his contemporaries. He is capable on the air of intense involvement in the most frivolous of antics, yet spends much of his time as a serious and dedicated citizen, as writer, scholar, and active participant in fields not remotely connected with humor, among them politics, civil rights, and the issue of capital punishment. Allen is unusual also in that he is both comedian *and* humorist.

The practice of reacting in terms of humor to events around him has apparently been second nature to Allen from his earliest days.

Was he born with the ability to be funny? He has said, "I came from a family of fast-talking, sarcastic Irish wits. My mother, Belle Montrose, was a vaudeville comedienne. Milton Berle calls her the funniest woman in vaudeville. I know of no case in which a really funny person grew up in a completely square environment. The ability to be funny is about 50 per cent heredity and 50 per cent environment."

That Allen at home is not unlike his public image should come as no surprise. His sense of the absurd, the ironic, the witty, or the plain zany prompts him to verbal or private reflections that can be triggered by almost any conceivable situation. Many of his ideas are not jokes in the traditional sense, and mostly they would be unsuitable for radio or television sketches. Passing one of Womrath's New York bookstores one day, he was heard to mutter, "The Womraths outgrabe." It would be asking too much of the mass TV audience to expect it to understand a pun involving a familiarity with Lewis Carroll's "Jabberwocky."

Allen's mind has been defined as a creative gag file, but editor Paul Krassner of *The Realist* has more accurately characterized it as a sort of Univac-in-reverse, gobbling up facts, figures, phrases, clichés, philosophy, and fantasy, and spewing them out, seemingly at random, in any number of unpredictable combinations. Once, when asked to improvise a poem, Steve started, "How can I leave thee? Let me count the ways."

The simplest question may lead to the unlikeliest answer. "Do they get your program in Boston?" a lady asked him one night in his TV studio.

"Well, they see it," he answered, "but they don't get it."

Another time a studio visitor said, "Mr. Allen, I've seen

you on television and you look five years younger in person."

"Thank you," said Allen. "By the way, how old is your set?"

Akin to Allen's penchant for literal interpretation is another form of humor that reflects his instinctive feeling for semantic nuances. A number of his best jokes have been based on grammatical or semantical misinterpretation of remarks made to him.

An exchange between Arlene Francis and Steve, during a radio interview:

ARLENE: Use [medical product] for itching, rashes, canker sores, and other skin irritations.

STEVE: Yes, it will cause all of them.

To an intoxicated friend who said, "Let me sit down here with you a minute and catch my breath," Allen replied, "Don't sit too close. I just caught it myself."

At a party at Nunnally Johnson's Beverly Hills home one evening, Johnson, Groucho Marx, and Allen became involved in a discussion of racial prejudice.

"I understand," Johnson said, "that one of the country clubs in town just took in a colored man."

"Really?" said Allen. "How many inches?"

Told that a somewhat lazy woman he knew would not be able to keep an appointment because she had "strained herself," Allen said, "Oh? Through what?"

One morning on her CBS radio show Lucille Ball asked Steve, "What do you think of working wives?"

"I don't know," he answered. "I've never worked any."

After watching him perform in a sketch, a boy in the audience asked Steve, "What do you do if you forget your part?"

"I comb my hair pompadour," replied Steve.

His wife, actress Jayne Meadows, has pointed out that Allen's offstage humor is of this same, quiet, reflective sort, usually based on a lightning-quick analysis of what *others* in the room are saying. He almost never is "on" in the Jerry Lewis sense, but is always tuned in. He never introduces a funny story, seldom stands up to do a bit (or *shtick*, to use a Yiddish word he has helped to popularize in the Gentile world). He does not do dialects, rarely plays practical jokes and demands no attention; rather, he adds spice to whatever conversation is taking place, either by making a point in a sudden and dramatic way, or else with some seemingly clownish observation with which he can relieve the tension that might otherwise engender an argument.

Though protean, his humor tends to be less acid than that of two comedians with whom he has often been compared, Groucho Marx and Fred Allen. "He is like neither," Jayne says, "but there is a sort of common middle ground among the three. Groucho, Fred, and Steve share the role of the seemingly disinterested philosophical quipster."

Allen has summed up eloquently the basic difference that separates a humorist like himself from the layman. The popular concept of the humorist or comedian, he says, is that he is a man who writes or does or says funny things. It is rarely realized that he is also a man to whom funny things happen. His experiences may not be inherently funnier than anyone else's, but he has a certain ultrasensitivity to the realities around him that enable him to perceive the comedic elements where a humorless person might miss them.

In his book *The Funny Men* Allen says, "I have seen and heard the most preposterously funny things and have been astonished to observe them pass unrecognized by others present. Their lack of receptivity is akin to having no ear for music.

"Men will accept almost any kind of criticism except the accusation that they have a deficient sense of humor. A man will admit to being a liar, a coward, a thief, an adulterer, a poor mechanic or a bad swimmer, but tell him that he has no sense of humor and you may as well have slandered his God, his flag or his mother.

"Even if he is civilized enough to pretend to parry the thrust with good grace, he will still secretly believe that he not only has a good sense of humor, but one vastly superior to most. He has a blind spot. His reluctance to evaluate himself correctly is all the more remarkable when we consider that not one man in a million can give you a meaningful answer as to what humor is or why he laughs. Even Freud never came to a complete conclusion when he tried to explore this mystery. He advanced a theory that laughter gives one a chance to gratify a forbidden impulse, such as illicit sexual craving or hostility against a spouse or an employer. He also pointed out that there is a sadistic emotional background for a lot of humor, but that still doesn't seem to answer the question. Max Eastman in *The Enjoyment of Laughter* points to the smiles of infants, who can't possibly have learned about sadism and cruelty. In any case, analysts and philosophers are apt to generalize too much about humor. They start out with comprehensive statements like 'all humor is . . .' and they're wrong right there, because *all* humor isn't any one thing. Sometimes they say surprise is a key ingredient in all humor, but it isn't. Most of us have heard things that we particularly like—say an album by Mike Nichols and Elaine May, or a dialect story by Myron Cohen—and we are eager to hear them again. The element of surprise can't possibly be there any more, but we still find the retelling hilariously funny."

Though his 1957 *Atlantic Monthly* article tended to treat all humor in terms of success or failure on television, this is—as I have observed—by no means the only medium for today's contemporary humor (least of all Allen's), any more than the vaudeville stage was the only major medium of yesterday. The various Allens to be found in the following chapters operate in at least half a dozen aural, visual, and written media: they include Allen the gagster, the college humorist, the ad-libber, the script writer, the journalist, the fiction writer, the autobiographer, the speechmaker, the interviewer, the letter writer, the punster, and the satirist. It would be hard to find any other funny man in American life today in whom one could find represented so complete a spectrum of humor and comedy.

The humor of Steve Allen preserved here provides a panchromatic view of the humor of the 1960s. In its variety and scope, its breadth and lack of pretension, it brings to mind a nineteenth-century definition offered by Lord Houghton in his *Memoir of Thomas Hood;*

> The sense of humour is the just balance of all the faculties of man, the best security against the pride of knowledge and the conceits of the imagination, the strongest inducement to submit with a wise and pious patience to the vicissitudes of human existence.

Through the multiformity of his wit I believe that Steve Allen has achieved that just balance more fully than any other public figure of our time.

2

THE EARLY YEARS

From reading his autobiography, *Mark It and Strike It,* one can perceive that, like most professional comedians, Allen was probably as funny at age five as he was ever to become. Although any performer can memorize jokes and develop an ability to deliver them, true comedians seem to be born rather than made. From his earliest years Allen was usually the clown in his schoolroom, the Peck's Bad Boy of his neighborhood, and the humorist in his social group.

Because his childhood was chaotic he early became adept at isolating the humorous element in a tragic or threatening situation. Perhaps this, basically, is all there is to a comedian anyway, and the professionals are those who render this service to those of us not very gifted at relieving emotional tension for ourselves.

The following recollection, although written when Allen was in his thirties, gives an insight into the sort of life he led during his teen-age years and suggests the attitude with which he approached inherently dangerous situations.

THE END OF THE WORLD

It was in the year of our Lord 1938—the last year, I briefly thought, that the Lord was to vouchsafe to us—

that my mother, my Aunt Margaret, and I (along with several million other Americans) went through an experience that not many people, proportionally speaking, will ever be privileged to share. We were on hand when the world came to an end.

The occasion, as the reader may have already divined, was the famous Orson Welles "War of the Worlds" broadcast. I have never before told the story of my own response to that broadcast because I have seen the reaction of those who were not victimized by Welles to those who were. It is the standard reaction of the level-headed citizen toward the crackpot. In my own defense, and in that of all the other crackpots who went squawking off into that unforgettable night like startled chickens, I would like to offer a word of explanation. Admittedly anybody who heard the entire Welles broadcast from beginning to end and believed a word of it should be put under observation. Unfortunately millions did not have that opportunity. Some of us missed the introduction of the program. For various reasons a great many people did not hear the first few minutes of the show. If some of these were in the mood for dance music they accepted what a randomly discovered orchestra was playing, lighted cigarettes, or picked up magazines and settled back to listen.

In a room on the eighth floor of the Hotel Raleigh, an ancient and run-down hostelry on Chicago's Near North Side that was our home that year, I was lying on the floor reading a book. Feeling in the mood for background music, I turned on my radio, fiddled with the dial until I heard dance music, and returned to my book. In the adjoining room Aunt Margaret and my mother were sitting on the bed playing cards.

After a moment the music was interrupted by a special "flash" from the CBS news department, the authenticity of which there was not the slightest reason to doubt, to the effect that from his observatory a scientist had just detected a series of mysterious explosions of a gaseous nature on the planet Mars. After this fascinating bit of intelligence, the announcer said, "And now we return you to the program in progress," and music was heard once more.

There soon followed a series of news flashes, each somewhat more exciting than its predecessor, that indicated that the strange explosions on Mars had caused a downpour of meteors in the general area of Princeton, New Jersey. By this time the music had been entirely forgotten, I had cast aside my book, and sitting cross-legged by the radio I listened with mounting horror while the smoothly functioning network news department went into action to bring America's radio listeners up-to-the-minute reports on what was transpiring in New Jersey.

More meteors had landed, it developed, and one of them in crashing into the earth had caused the death of several hundred people. CBS at once dispatched a crew to the scene and it was not long before first-hand reports began coming in. Up to now there was not the slightest reason for those of us who had tuned in the dance music to question the truth of a word that had been broadcast. This granted, there was no particular reason for being suspicious of what immediately followed.

With disbelief rising in his throat, a specialevents man on the scene near Princeton reported that one of the Martian meteors appeared to be no meteor at all, but some sort of spaceship. It actually appeared, he said, although one could scarcely believe one's ears, that this giant blob of metal, half buried in the New Jersey mud, was not a blind, inert fragment shrugged off by some burly planet hurtling through infinity. Rather, it appeared to have been "fashioned" somehow. Bolts and hinges were in evidence, and the National Guard had roped off the area, allowing no one near the gargantuan hulk. This move, as far as one could determine, was simply a formal precaution, for it seemed starkly clear that even if—fantastic thought—some strange form of life had made the flight from Mars inside the meteor it could certainly not have survived the crushing impact when the weird craft plunged into the earth.

By this time my mother and Aunt Mag were huddled around the speaker with me, wide-eyed. The contents of the news broadcast were inherently unbelievable, and yet we had it on the authority of the Columbia Broadcasting System that such things were actually happening.

But if our credulity had been strained up to now, it had yet to face the acid test. The network now presented an army officer who made a dignified plea for calm, stating that the National Guard and the New Jersey police had the situation completely in hand. He requested that motorists give the area a wide berth until matters had been satisfactorily dealt with and concluded with a few words conveying his complete assurance that it would be only a matter of hours until order had been restored. But it at once developed that his confidence was badly misplaced.

The network interrupted his sedate sermon with another report from the scene of the trouble, frankly emotional in nature, which confirmed the suspicions of some authorities that there might possibly be life of some kind inside one of the rockets. Fearful listeners were now treated to the benumbing description by a patently frightened newsman of the emergence of strange leathery creatures from the spaceship. I suppose if one has been convinced that there is life on Mars it matters not whether Martians be leathery, rubbery, or made of Philadelphia Cream Cheese. The description of grotesque monsters by this time seemed in no detail too fantastic; what *was* fantastic was that there were any creatures in the rocket at all. Their slavering mouths, jellylike eyes, and the devastating fire they directed toward the soldiers who dared stand and face them were all minor, almost unimportant, details, and even now they are not clear in my mind.

The National Guard troops who had been dispatched to the scene were massacred almost at once by the huge interplanetary invaders (there were several of them now, for other ships were landing) and in the confusion of the battle the network's facilities were impaired and its Johnny-on-the-spot was cut off in midsentence.

CBS, however, was equal to the occasion. Civic and governmental spokesmen were rushed to microphones; dutifully—and ineffectually, as it turned out—they instructed the populace not to panic. An airplane was sent up over the trouble area and the network continued its blow-by-blow description from the clouds. My mother, my aunt, and I didn't wait to hear any more. We looked at each other, not knowing what to say.

"Good God," Aunt Mag gasped, her face pale, "what's going on?"

"I don't know," I said. "What do you think we ought to do?"

"There's only one thing *to* do," my mother responded. "We can all go over to church and wait there to see what happens." She referred to the Holy Name Cathedral, not many blocks from our hotel.

"I don't know if that's such a good idea," I said. "There might be crowds."

Just then we heard the word "Chicago" on the radio. "More spaceships have been reported," a voice intoned. "Observers have seen them over Cleveland, Detroit, and Chicago."

"Jesus, Mary, and Joseph!" Aunt Mag shouted. "We'll be killed right here in this hotel!" She ran back into the other room and grabbed her coat.

"What are you doing, Maggie?" my mother said.

"What do you think?" Mag said. "We can't stay here and be killed. Let's get out of here."

"You're right," Mother said. "We'll go over to the church. Who has the key to the room?"

"Who the hell cares about locking the door?" Mag said. "It doesn't matter now."

I was putting my coat on, still too shocked to say much. Oddly enough, and this I recall quite clearly, my predominant emotion was not fear, but blank stupefaction. I remember saying "Gosh," idiotically, over and over, and frowning and shaking my head from side to side. I couldn't believe it, and yet I had to, on the basis of years of conditioning. CBS had never lied to me before.

Aunt Mag was still fluttering around the room. The door was now ajar, but she was like a bird that, with its cage opened, doesn't know just where to fly.

"What are you looking for?" Mother asked.

"My glasses," Mag said.

"You're not going to have time to read anything, Maggie," Mother told her. "Just get your hat and let's get out of here!"

"If I don't need my glasses what good is my hat?" said my aunt, unaccountably.

"Never mind," said my mother. "Let's go." They both stopped to look at me. Perhaps I was a bit pale.

"Are you all right?" my mother asked.

"Gosh," I said, resourcefully, and we headed for the door. By this time people all over the nation were reacting similarly. Many stayed glued to their radios and heard the reassuring conclusion to the program, but millions, like us, rushed off wildly. They had not heard the introduction to the broadcast and they did not stay to be reassured by its finale.

Police stations, newpapers, and churches were badly shaken by the first wave of frightened, fleeing citizens. In one New Jersey town a terrified man rushed into the First Baptist Church during evening services and announced that the end was at hand. The pastor made a futile attempt to quiet his flock by leading them in a prayer for deliverance.

Switchboards at CBS stations from coast to coast were clogged for hours by callers, some angry, some panicky.

In New York's Harlem more than one police station was besieged by terror-stricken men and women seeking refuge.

Conscience-plagued sinners all over the country began making efforts to return stolen money, confess undisclosed sins, and right old wrongs. People in houses rushed into the streets, and people on the streets rushed into houses. About this time Welles and the members of his cast, glancing toward the control room of their studio, perceived that it was crowded with policemen. They must have finished the program in a state almost as disturbed as that of many of their listeners. Needless to say, none of this was known to us at the time.

"Button your overcoat, Steve," my mother said. "You'll catch cold when we go out."

This remark did not at the moment strike any of us as amusing. I buttoned my overcoat and we hurried out to let the hotel in on our secret tonight—tomorrow the world.

My mother and aunt ran down the hall and I followed at a slower pace, not because I was trying to maintain a shred of discretion but because I was too stunned to move with speed. Rounding a corner in the hall, we burst suddenly upon a dignified-looking young woman with a little girl in her arms.

"Run for your life!" my mother cried at the woman, at the same time jabbing a shaky but determined finger at the elevator button. In response the woman looked at her with no expression whatsoever.

"Pick up your child and come with us!" Aunt Mag shouted, wild-eyed. The woman paused a moment and then laughed right in her face.

Mag was outraged. "Oh yes," she sputtered with withering sarcasm. "Go ahead and laugh! But for the sake of that dear baby in your arms don't you laugh!" At this the young woman drew back in some alarm, evidently concluding that she was confronted by three violently deranged people who might do her physical harm. She looked at me questioningly, and I felt that some sort of explanation was due her.

"We just heard on the radio," I said, "that there's something up in the sky."

The merest flicker of bemusement crossed her face, but she did not speak. It was clear that she was hovering between two alternatives: either we were a trio of incredibly inventive and determined practical jokesters or we were insane. The third possibility—that there might actually be something up in the sky—apparently was never given serious consideration. Instead she shifted the child in her arms to a more secure position and retreated a few steps down the hall, walking backward so as to keep an eye on us. But my aunt was not to accord this move the honor of understanding. She moved angrily toward the woman and her right hand pointed up toward the heavens. She must have looked like a witch calling down a curse.

"You ought to get down on your *knees,*" she shouted —like a complete nut, "instead of laughing at people! We're going to church to pray and that's what you ought to be doing right this minute, *praying!*"

Before the woman could interpret this admonition a soft whir and a click announced that the elevator had reached our floor. A moment later the door slid back and the smiling face of the colored operator greeted us. Never have I seen a smile fade so fast. If this scene were to be enacted in a motion picture this man's part would be played by Manton Moreland, who would undoubtedly be called upon to open his eyes wide with fear and say, "Feet, get movin!" In any event the violence with which we dashed into the elevator convinced the operator that all was not well. My mother's first words confirmed his suspicions, I'm sure.

"Hurry up and take us down," she gasped. "They're up in the sky!"

"Who is?" asked the young man, aghast.

"How do we know who is?" my aunt shouted. "But you'd better get out of this hotel right now while you've still got the chance!"

"Yes, ma'am!" he whispered, withdrawing completely to his corner of the elevator. For perhaps ten seconds he regarded us warily, holding the car-control handle at full speed, then, torn between fear and curiosity, he succumbed to the latter. "What did you say the matter was?" he said, frowning.

Aunt Mag's patience was exhausted. How many times did you have to explain things to people? "They're up in the sky," she repeated. "Haven't you been listening to the radio?"

"No, ma'am."

"Well, you'd better do something, let me tell you. The radio just said they're up over Chicago, so you'd better run for your life!"

I am sure that if the elevator operator had been convinced that an interplanetary invasion was underway he would have faced the issue as bravely as the next man. But instead he apparently concentrated on the idea that he was cooped up in a tiny cubicle with three dangerous lunatics and as a result became positively petrified. Fortunately, for his nervous system, we arrived at the main floor at this point. Convulsively he yanked the door release and shrank back against the wall as we thundered past him into the lobby.

Though we had met with icy disbelief twice in quick
succession we were still ill-prepared for the sight that
now greeted us. The lobby, which we had expected to
find in absolute turmoil, was a scene of traditional palm-
shaded, lobbylike calm. Nowhere was there evidence of
the panic that we had come to accept as the norm in a
few short minutes. Aggravatingly, people were sitting
about, smoking cigars, reading newspapers, speaking in
subdued tones, or dozing peacefully in thick leather
chairs.

It had been our intention to sweep through the lobby
and proceed right across Dearborn Street, pausing only in
the event that a sudden spaceship attack should force us
to take cover, but something about the tranquility around
the registration desk of the hotel presented a challenge
we did not feel strong enough to resist. Indeed, we felt
it our duty to warn the unfortunate souls who thought
all was well that they were about to witness ultimate
disaster.

The elevator man peered after us from what was now
the safety of his cage as we raced to confront the blasé
desk clerk. "Is something wrong?" this worthy said
quietly, evidently hoping that if something *were* amiss
he could contain the area of alarm within his immediate
vicinity.

"Well," said my aunt with a contemptuous sneer, "it's
the end of the world, that's all that's wrong!"

The clerk's face was an impenetrable mask, although
after a moment he permitted a suggestion of disdain to
appear on it. I started to explain that on the radio—and
then in some clear, calm corner of my mind I heard
something. It was a radio, it was making soft sounds in

a corner of the lobby, and the sounds were not the sort a radio should be making at a time of world-wide crisis. The sounds, as a matter of fact, were of a commercial nature. Some other announcer on some other station was extolling the virtues of a brand of tomato soup.

A wave of shock passed through me as, in the instant, I saw things as they really were. Turning to my mother, I began speaking very fast, explaining exactly what had happened. For a split second she wavered, hoping, yet fearing, and then for her, too, the ice broke.

Light, followed by painful embarrassment, also dawned on Aunt Mag. Like bewildered sheep we retreated, excruciatingly aware that all heads were turned toward us, that the clerk was smiling at us in a frightfully patronizing way, and that never again as long as we lived would we be able to walk through that lobby without casting our eyes to the floor.

"We'll have to move out of this place," my mother said.

Our next reaction, upon us before we could even stagger back into the elevator, was one of wild hilarity bordering on hysteria. We laughed until our sides ached and tears poured down our cheeks. We fell into heavy chairs and laughed some more, and at long last we pulled ourselves together, still shrieking with laughter, and started back toward our quarters. We laughed so hard going up in the elevator that I don't recall the elevator operator's reactions; I'm sure he must have assumed we were still nutty as three fruit cakes, if no longer dangerous.

We spent a restless night, alternately laughing and saying, "We'll never be able to face all those people." The next day on the way to school I glanced at a newspaper headline and knew that we had not been alone.

COLLEGE HUMOR

"When as a young man I was working in Arizona," Allen recalls, "I used to practice ad-libbing by pretending to be on the air as I drove around in my car, describing the passing scenery to an imaginary audience. I think the exercise was beneficial to me, however unnerving it may have been to local pedestrians."

Actually, radio was Allen's third area of activity. While he was studying at Drake University in Des Moines, Iowa, and during both high school and college attendance in Phoenix, Arizona, he occasionally played local gigs as a professional pianist. Around the same time, his first attempts at humorous writing achieved print, through the *Drake University Bulldog*. The following is a poem written during his freshman year there, in 1941.

The subject was a football game played in a driving rainstorm. At that time the nineteen-year-old Allen was assigned to write straight sports stories but decided to do one in verse.

"WASHINGTON DROWNS DRAKE, 12–0!"

'Twas a rainy autumn evening, and a goodly crowd was
    there
Which well nigh drowned as torrents formed Niagaras
    in the air.

Oh, the boys who led the cheering heard it turn to croak
and cough,

And when the team picked up five yards they had to
scrape it off.

For the mud was on the football, and a dozen times the
huddle

Had to be detoured because someone near drowned
beneath a puddle.

Yes, they stumbled and they fumbled, and they couldn't
see the ball.

Why, they gained less with the end-around than the
Australian crawl.

The referee had troubles on the slipp'ry, swishy sward,

Three times he blew the whistle, and declared "Man
overboard!"

The cheerers wetly shouted as the finish nearer drew,

"Yea boat, yea boat, water we gonna dew?"

But the Bears splashed to a touchdown, to the Bulldog's
great chagrin,

Though the score might have been different if the tide
had not come in.

For there was a crucial moment in the second half, you
know,

When the ball was on the twenty—drown two and three
to go.

A center plunge—a fumble—a pile-up—and a shout!

Six men fell in a puddle, but only five came out.

Oh, they're looking still for Harvey, they're looking still
for Jim,

For it seems the lad went in the game, but never learned
    to swim.
The Bulldog victory ship was up the creek without a
    rudder,
But we'll be kind to all the boys, each man is someone's
    mudder.

A subject for satire that appealed to Allen's sense of
the ridiculous during his college years was the radio soap
opera.

"I occasionally used to listen," he says, "perhaps for
the same morbid reasons that make us watch automobile accidents. I noticed each day's program was pref-
aced by a lengthy recapitulation of recent events, and
that unless you had really been keeping up with the story
these recaps were of very little help.

"One day on the old *Smile Time* show, I did a short
routine, originally written while I was at college, giving
my version of an announcer bringing the occasional listener up to date."

YESTERDAY, YOU'LL REMEMBER

Yesterday, you'll remember, Agatha paled when Roger
entered the library. It seemed as if only days before he
had gone out of her life, vowing never to return. And
now, here they were strolling along the beach, arm in
arm. As they climbed the flagpole David spoke to her,
softly. And it seemed that never had a hamburger tasted
so good.

Flinging the book into the fire, Elizabeth stood for a

moment, poised against the window, then—with a suddenness that took Richard's breath away—she strode to the table and began putting the puppies back into the suitcase.

It was then that they both saw the thing. A tiny drop of blood on the man's shirt front. It could mean only one thing. And not a drop of liquor in the house.

As Helen pulled the speedy, low-slung Mercedes McCambridge into the drive-in, she felt a sudden sense of weariness, and almost without thinking threw back the covers and got out of bed. When the phone rang she let it ring for a long while, and then—very carefully—she spat out the tobacco, vowing never to return.

Would Dr. Carvel arrive on time? Samantha did not know, and cared less. Not for her, ever again, the long walks in the country. Suddenly, lashing out with the lash she always carried, she slapped William full in the face. Then, primly confident, she turned on her heel, let it run for a while, and then turned it off.

As the curtain opened, a nervous titter ran through the audience. Dr. Gillespie whipped out a titter pistol and shot it.

Now, on with today's installment . . .

EARLY RADIO

In the following pages Allen reminisces about his early days at the local radio station in Arizona, where, after leaving school, he acquired his basic training in broadcasting.

THE OLD RADIO DAYS

The old local radio days were a lot of fun, particularly if you worked at a small station. I spent three years at KOY in Phoenix, Arizona—then a CBS outlet—and loved every minute of it.

There was always something happening at KOY and if excitement didn't regularly present itself, why, the announcers or other staff members cooked up something just to keep life interesting. As chief continuity writer for the station there was one practical joke I was in a peculiarly advantageous position to perpetrate and I used to spring it on one or another of my fellow announcers every few months. Basically the gag simply involved slipping a phony commercial into the poor guy's announcement book, but the method of doing so was ingenious. You see, no announcer would fall for it if you just handed him a piece of off-beat copy, so I had to resort to the cleverness of a master forger.

Selecting some dog-eared commercial that had been broadcast scores of times, I would retype it very carefully on an identical piece of KOY stationery, except that the last few lines would make no sense whatever. For example:

Say, men, if you want your friends to admire the cut of your clothes be sure to visit the Thew Tailors at 429 Washington Boulevard. Thew is noted for the high quality of his workmanship and thousands of satisfied customers will assure you that wearing a Thew suit is just like sticking your hand into a wet pumpkin and getting the juice up your sleeve. Yes, friends, eating a bowl of chocolate-covered sardines while punching your grandfather in the mouth will bring home the thrill of wearing a suit of clothes that . . .

Having written a pageful of such nonsense, I would then rub the sheet of paper on the floor to make it resemble the dog-eared and finger-stained commercials in the morning schedule book, rubber-stamp the back, forge a lot of initials to make it appear that the copy had been approved and read dozens of times, slip the phony commercial into the chosen slot, and then set my alarm at home to wake me about two minutes before the announcement was scheduled to be read the following day.

The alarm would awaken me, say, at 7:25. At 7:27 the luckless mark would launch into his pitch, and by 7:30 I'd fall asleep again, laughing. The thing that made it all possible is that the average announcer really hasn't a very clear idea what he's talking about. Most announcers who are experienced seldom *think* at all while they are reciting. Years of parroting other people's thoughts have conditioned them to blabbing almost any sort of gobble-degook without becoming involved emotionally or intellectually. When I used to listen to my colleagues on the morning shift they would often read seven or eight lines of my absurd prose before they caught on. It was more fun than a barrelful of complaints from angry sponsors.

THE SECRET I CAN NO LONGER LIVE WITH

Recently the House Special Subcommittee on Legislative Oversight charged that some radio stations had rigged man-on-the-street interviews "in a systematic vilification of persons and companies."

Since ours is a day of breast-beating and coming-clean, I hereby confess that once in Phoenix, Arizona, years ago, I shamelessly rigged a man-on-the-street show, though not for purposes of vilification. The crime was committed in broad daylight at a supermarket near radio station KOY. My accomplice was Bill Lester, a fellow announcer. The circumstances were as follows.

Bill and I were doing a fifteen-minute program called "How Do You Vote?" the elements of which were simple. A team of announcers would go to a busy spot and take turns interviewing passers-by. After chatter of an introductory nature came the question: "For whom are you going to vote in the coming election? And why?"

That year the presidential contestants were Franklin Roosevelt and Thomas Dewey; on the afternoon in question Bill and I were soliciting endorsements in a grocery store. Bill conducted the first interview while I induced an elderly woman to be interrogated second. Then, while I pumped this kindly soul for her political opinions, Bill quietly rounded up his next prospect. All went swimmingly until about halfway through the program when I looked up and noticed that there was no one left to interview. Bill was just concluding a chat with a middle-aged man and I motioned frantically to stretch the conversation. But the man had nothing more to say and had to be dismissed.

With hand signals I attempted to convey the dimensions of our predicament to Bill, and then was suddenly seized by an inspiration. "Bill," I said unctuously, "I have another guest for you, Mr. Walter Kline." Bill's head spun around looking for Kline, but I promptly resolved his confusion by saying, "How do you do?" in what I hoped was the high, quavery voice of a citizen of very advanced years. Bill caught on right away.

"Pleased to meet you, Mr. Kline," he said. "Tell me, where do you live?"

"Oh, out on Twenty-fourth Street," I said tiredly.

"I see," Bill said. "All right, you know the name of the program. Whom do you plan to vote for in the coming presidential election?"

"Oh," I said, "I'm pretty much of a Dewey man."

"Really?" said Bill. "And why is that?"

"Well," I said, "I think it's time for a change."

"Is that your only reason for preferring Dewey?" Bill asked.

"Yes," I said. "That's about the size of it."

"Thank you, Mr. Kline," Bill said. "And now, Steve, I believe you want to interview our next guest."

"Thank you, Bill," I said in my own voice. "We have a gentleman right here. What is your name, sir?"

"My name," said Bill Lester in a strange, choked tone, "is A. K. Johnson. I'm from Tucson."

"Then how," I said, "do you happen to be doing your grocery shopping here in Phoenix this afternoon?"

We went on that way for another seven or eight minutes, conscientiously splitting the votes, half for Dewey and half for Roosevelt. We said nothing unkind about either candidate so I presume the House Special Subcommittee will not be calling us. But I feel much better for having made a clean breast of the whole thing.

3

HOLLYWOOD TO NEW YORK

By 1944—after an army hitch—Allen had made the move to Hollywood. In 1946 and '47, along with another former Phoenix announcer named Wendell Noble, he did a daily quarter-hour comedy program called *Smile Time* on the coast-to-coast Mutual radio network. These two years were what he now calls "practically a college course in comedy," in that he and Noble had to write their own scripts, which forced them not only to create new material but—necessity being the mother of their rather quickly exhausted invention—to learn practically every old joke that they could dig up out of gag books and humor magazines.

When *Smile Time* ended in 1948 Allen and Noble found themselves unable to get work as a team. Noble went back to announcing and singing.

Being fired by the Mutual Broadcasting System was clearly the luckiest thing that ever happened to Allen professionally. Although *Smile Time* had been a successful program it was conventional in format, completely written and rehearsed, and therefore presented Allen with no opportunity to ad-lib. In fact at this point in his career he was not even aware that he *could* ad-lib. Purely to keep the wolf away from the door he accepted an offer from Station KNX, the Hollywood CBS outlet, to

HOLLYWOOD TO NEW YORK

do a disc-jockey program from 11:30 P.M. to midnight five nights a week, although at the time he regarded the venture as a step in the wrong direction. After all, for two years—with Noble—he had had his own coast-to-coast comedy program. Now: a lowly, local, late-night disc jockey. The injustice of it all! But Allen's imagination proceeded at once to sabotage the station's plans for his time slot. He began talking more and playing records less until after a few months he had converted the program into something new not only to himself but to radio generally.

One night something happened that brought about the birth of not only the Steve Allen now known to the nation but also of the entire late-night, ad-lib format subsequently popularized on TV not only by Allen but by Jack Paar, Johnny Carson, Les Crane, Merv Griffin, and others. In late 1948 the length of his program on Station KNX was doubled, but his salary was not proportionately increased. At these prices he did not feel inclined to write an extra half hour of comedy every night. Instead he embarked on a policy of interviewing guests from the motion picture and record fields.

One evening Doris Day, scheduled for a guest interview, failed to appear. "I had about twenty-five minutes of open air time left," Allen recalls. "I was on the air live, and I'd used up everything I'd written. So I just grabbed a microphone and began to wander among the forty or fifty people in the studio, interviewing them at random. It got bigger laughs than anything I'd ever done before. I thought to myself, 'I've been doing this sort of thing at home all my life . . . now they'll let me do it in public and pay me for it.'"

Friends began dropping by the studio to watch him perform. When he said something funny they laughed. Listeners heard the laughter and wrote in asking if they, too, could join the party. The process snowballed fast, with the result that within six months Allen's night-owl program was doing standing-room-only business at the largest CBS studio in Hollywood. The program ran for three years—1948, '49, and '50—and was far and away the most popular local radio show in the history of Los Angeles. Audiences stood in line for two and three hours to get front-row seats at the nightly impromptu sessions. To this day thousands of Angelenos remember the broadcast with a special fondness. Al Jolson called it "the best show on the air." Other performers were equally lavish in their praise. Some of the greats of the entertainment world—such as Fannie Brice and Ethel Barrymore—would rarely go to sleep at night without listening to the youthful Allen.

Late in 1950, CBS decided that Allen rated exposure on coast-to-coast television. Because at that time there was no method of transmitting transcontinental programs from California, he had to move to New York.

Manhattan, Allen found, "is a place where funny things happen . . . well, maybe the whole world is, but to me it seems that *more* funny things happen in New York. Here is an example of what I mean about New York. One night I was coming out of Luchow's restaurant down on Fourteenth Street when a vagrant came up to me and made the traditional pitch for a dime. As it happened that was the exact amount of change I had in my pocket, the next smallest article of exchange being a five-dollar bill. So I gave him the dime and he lurched off into the night.

"Out of idle curiosity I turned, after a moment, to look back at him. He was standing under a neon sign that said TEN CENTS A DANCE. He paused a moment, straightened his shoulders, and then marched upstairs, presumably to dance his dime away. Now, you've got to admit that that story comes under the heading of where-but-in-New York."

The young comic's first couple of years in New York proved erratic as CBS shifted him into a variety of morning, afternoon, and evening time slots. He substituted for Arthur Godfrey, became a regular *What's My Line?* panelist in 1952, and for a year and a half was the star of a Saturday night show called *Songs for Sale*.

Though the early New York years were by no means the most successful or productive of his career, they generated many hilarious moments. There is no record of most of the material involved, since both the television and radio programs were predominantly ad-lib. The examples that follow are transcripts of a few typical interviews from this period.

A WILD NIGHT AT CHANDLER'S

I

By 1953 Allen had become New York's first-choice for any ad-lib radio or TV assignment. He officiated at scores of banquets and luncheons during this period, appeared on countless panel and discussion shows, and filled in for various radio interviewers on their nights off.

The following transcript was made from a recording of a mad, unforgettable three-hour broadcast he conducted on the night of January 11, 1953, from Chandler's restaurant in Manhattan. Barry Gray had taken the evening off and asked Allen to replace him. It was a bitterly cold Sunday night and Steve was moderately exhausted when he arrived at the restaurant, having already done two television programs that same evening, *This Is Show Business* and *What's My Line?*

His unexpected appearance at the microphone was greeted by applause, made somewhat warmer by the fact that a number of those at ringside tables were under the influence of spirits. Although Allen can, when he wishes, conduct serious interviews, there are times when he obviously makes the choice to cast reason to the winds and instead depend upon pure whimsy, effrontery, free association, and lightning-quick, outlandish play-on-words. . . . Clearly, this was one of those times.

His guests were Jim Moran, the fabled publicist, Tom Scott, a folk balladeer, Bob Carroll, a popular singer, Bill Silbert, a New York disc jockey, and assorted droppers-by.

To the opening applause Allen responded, "Please! No public demonstrations. I'm going to be here for three hours, regardless of your attitude."

This announcement was greeted by more applause.

"Well," Allen said, shrugging, "have it your way. This is the Barry Gray Show, but Barry isn't here tonight." At this moment a waiter approached and placed a cup of coffee on Allen's table.

"There's a waiter here, however," Steve reported. "What is your name, my good man?"

WAITER: Jack. Jack.

ALLEN: Jack-Jack, eh? It's nice to have both of you here tonight, Jack. Thanks for the coffee. Well, we certainly have a packed house here tonight. I mean it looks like a packing house here tonight.

We have a pleasant party of folks here right in front and we'll be talking to them a little later. Now you people can get nervous. Coffee cups begin jiggling, perspiration breaks out on the brow.

I guess I'll be doing the commercials tonight. How soon do I have to do one?

I don't want you to feel that I'm picking on you, Jack, because I ask you questions like this. But that's the way it's going to be. No commercials till 12:30?

You folks who are seated at the tables here will find little cards on your tables. If you have any comments write your ideas down on these little pieces of paper and I'll collect all these pieces of paper and burn them, because the program is going to be overcrowded as it is.

We have quite a few guests coming over tonight. Jim Moran. You know Jim Moran, sir? You're a Canadian? He's very big up there. You will know him before you leave tonight, unless you leave soon. Then you can hear it in your car.

Your car is in Canada? Well, there's a plane leaving in about twenty minutes.

How often do you get to New York, sir?

CANADIAN: Quite often, on business.

ALLEN: What do you do?

CANADIAN: I'm in the steel business.

ALLEN: Well, we all do a little of that, I suppose. What did you have here tonight?

CANADIAN: So far, two scotches.

ALLEN: And nothing in between them for a sandwich? Well, I hope you're enjoying yourself. *Somebody* is eating at your table so you'll be in good hands. What was that lady over there saying a few minutes ago? You saw me on television? I was on *What's My Line?* tonight. Do you purchase any of the products that the program advertises? Stopette, you know, the thing you squeeze? I was listening to the girl announcer tonight. They have an attractive young lady who does the commercials. I like that line where she says, "*Poof,* there goes perspiration!" I think there is a market right now for a product called Perspiration that gets rid of "poof."

Here comes a new group. Hello! You folks have been to a dinner, have you? I see. And you're here to get rid of it? Where were you, sir?

MAN: I don't remember the name—at the Waldorf at a Yeshiva thing.

ALLEN: What was the purpose?

MAN: To raise funds.

ALLEN: To pay for the dinner, I presume.

ANOTHER MAN: To raise funds for a Yeshiva. Eddie Fisher was the star of the evening.

ALLEN: Eddie's in town, eh?

That's not the most intelligent question I've ever asked but it will do. Somebody sent me up a note that says, "What do you think of Cinerama?" I haven't seen the new version, I saw it originally with Richard Dix and Irene Dunne many years ago. Don't explain it. *Cimar-*

ron. I know what I'm talking about, I just want *you* to do a little thinking.

Somebody was telling me the other day about two fellows who went to see Cinerama. The first shot, I'm informed, makes you feel like you're in a roller coaster. Well, these two fellows are sitting there in the theater and suddenly one puts his hand over his brow and he says, "Ooh, Harry, I'm sick. I'll see you later." The other fellow says, "Will you sit down? I waited two months for these tickets. Now, just sit there and don't act like a child."

The first guy says, "I'm sorry, I don't want to embarrass you but I have to get out of here. I'm very sick." The other fellow says, "Now, wait a minute. We paid good money for these seats. Don't embarrass me. Just act like a man and sit down."

So the fellow gives it another try. He sits there about five minutes and all of a sudden he turns white and he says, "I'm awful sorry, I don't want to cause any trouble. You go right ahead and enjoy the picture. I've got to get out of here right now. I'm sick as a dog." So he stands up and the other fellow says, "Will you sit down? You're going to fall out of this thing and get killed."

Wasn't that a cute story? Funny part of it was I *did* fall out!

And while I was lying there Barry said, "Will you replace me this Sunday?"

We have some more guests coming in. Rick Keller is going to be here. Say, do you know who Rick Keller is?

MAN: Yes.

ALLEN: Who is he? He must be somebody very important, and the simple fact that *I* don't know who he is doesn't mean a thing because you'd be surprised how much I don't know.

It says here that he's a motorboat-racing champ from Detroit. He has a hydroplane, the *Bevwyn,* which he takes around the country and campaigns in. What is he running for? Well, we'll find out.

We've established a mystery now which we'll all stay awake until we hear cleared up a bit later.

Bill Pearsall is going to be here? Do you know Bill Pearsall? No.

Maybe he's a friend of Rick Keller's. Anyway, Bill Pearsall will be here. He's a publicity man for the motor-boat show. He *is* a friend of Rick Keller's.

Here's another note. It says, "Dear Steve, work very close to the mike and a little louder." If it were any closer it would be *behind* me. Would you like me to swallow it?

This is WMCA in New York. Where are we on the dial? Does anybody know? You say 1010, and *you* say 570. Do I hear 1250? It's going, going, sold to the man for 1010! WMCA is 1010? No, that's W-M-G-M, the voice of the stars, that's 1010. This is WMCA, the voice of the *extras.* More notes are coming in. This one says, "They are here."

II

Oh, *Rick* and *Bill* are here. Where are Rick and Bill? Where are Bob and Ray? Where are Gallagher and Shean, Finn and Haddie?

Well, it's nice to know you're here even if we don't know which of the many people who are here you are. Are you Rick Keller? Rick, come over here and we'll rectify a very awkward situation. I've always wanted to talk to a motorboat-racing champ. Ladies and gentlemen, Rick Keller. Rick, you say you have a hydroplane?

KELLER: Well, Steve, I've been down at the Harwood Trophy here in New York for four years.

ALLEN: What's the Harwood trophy?

KELLER: That is probably the most difficult race of all. It's put on by the powerboat people. The race starts at Seventy-second Street and goes around Manhattan Island.

ALLEN: In the water, I presume? What do you drive?

KELLER: We call it a boat. It's just a matter of six or seven square inches of surface on the water. Most of your support is through the air when you get these things going.

ALLEN: I've never seen anything very fast going up and down the Hudson River. When do you fellows do it?

KELLER: The course here in New York is pretty rough. The average speeds here are way down because the water is . . . ah . . .

ALLEN: Way up?

KELLER: It's up, and it's tough on the boats. Out where I come from we get smooth water now and then.

ALLEN: How do you smooth water? Do you put oil on it, or iron it?

KELLER: We get out there at four o'clock in the morning, before we go home.

ALLEN: Where have you been all night that you get out there at four in the morning before you go home?

KELLER: Maybe my wife, Beth, is listening. I'm not going to talk.

ALLEN: Does *she* drive, or fly, or scoot, or whatever it is you do?

KELLER: She is probably the greatest supporter I've got in the game.

ALLEN: That's nice. What with her and the air you should have a lot of support, and that's what we all need I suppose. How did you get into this game, Rick?

KELLER: I met a guy from the West Coast by the name of Stan Dollar. He brought his boat to Detroit and needed some help on it. The thing broke down the first five minutes he was on the race course. And I, trying to be a good guy, went out and helped him along with his gearbox and before I woke up to what was going on I had the boat myself and I've been in it now for four years.

ALLEN: How did that happen? Did you fall into his gearbox? . . . Are you independently wealthy, Rick? Might you be called a wealthy young sportsman?

KELLER: I like to have fun. I'm not wealthy, but I found out how to do it cheaply. That's the secret in the boating game, too.

ALLEN: Yes, we're all trying to find that out. How fast have you gone?

KELLER: I've got an honest ninety miles an hour to my credit. I think that we're on a new beam in the game now.

ALLEN: New beam? In the game now? What do you mean, Rick—new beam in the game now?

KELLER: Well, this hobby has gone too far with me. I started out as just a mechanic and then I got into the driving stage and now I'm a builder. As a matter of fact, my winter will be taken up building three seven-liter boats.

ALLEN: What's a seven-liter boat?

KELLER: Seven-liter designates the displacement of the engine and that's our limitation in the sport. Seven-liters converted over is 427 cubic inches.

ALLEN: I see. [*Pause*] What's a seven-liter boat?

KELLER: That's a one-seater, and it goes too damned fast for me.

ALLEN: Tell us a little bit about the motorboat show at Grand Central Palace.

KELLER: I'd like to give some real credit to Joe Choate.

ALLEN: Joe who?

KELLER: Choate—that's C-H-O-A-T-E.

ALLEN: Oh, fine. That's F-I-N-E.

KELLER: He has put together probably the greatest assembly of cruiser and sailboat hulls that the American people will ever see.

ALLEN: The hull you say. Is Bill Pearsall over there with you?

KELLER: Yes, Bill is here.

ALLEN: Why don't you come up and I'll ask you a couple of questions, too, if I may. What's the big news at the moment at the show? Any new records been broken, or anybody gone down or anything?

PEARSALL: Recordwise, it's a big show. Attendance-wise, lots of people.

ALLEN: It's nice that everything is so wise. How long will it be running?

PEARSALL: Through next Saturday.

ALLEN: I'm through next Saturday myself. How did you get into motorboat promotion, Bill?

PEARSALL: Steve, you know if you play around with boats a long while—

ALLEN: You drown.

Well, fellows, I want to thank you both for coming in and, all kidding aside—that's a thing you have to say on the radio when you've loused up a whole interview—you say "all kidding aside," and that's supposed to make it all right. You spoil everybody's evening, but, all kidding aside—nice to see you both.

Commercial? Oh, North American Air Coach. I'll read what they have written here and see if it makes sense. One of Barry's sponsors is North American Air Coach. There are two very good reasons why more people fly North American than ever before. I'll enumerate these reasons for you: Number One and Number Two.

No, they have it written here. One, North American's dependability and service, and, Two, North American offers the lowest airline fares (which is a good straight line, but I'd better leave it alone). You can go to California for eighty-eight dollars. You sit *inside* the plane for twenty dollars extra.

Actually it's a great deal. All kidding aside. Chicago, nonstop, twenty-four dollars. If you want to get off at Cincinnati, that's tough. You go to Chicago and look at the money you've saved.

North American's rate to Miami is thirty-nine dollars with a 10 per cent discount on a return trip. So you've *got* to come back, whether you like it or not. They'll drag you right out of your bed at the Eden Roc and you get on that plane and you'll come back because it's a great saving.

There's a gracious stewardess service. When you see the stewardess you'll say "Gracious!"

And there's a free ticket delivery at no additional cost. Only a small charge.

So schedule your flight now with the oldest and largest air-coach system in the country. The planes are the oldest and largest.

And space is limited. So call Judson 6-2100 right now. Or we have another number: Chickering 6-cha-la-cha-la.

Remember the numbers. Why don't you write them down in lipstick on your forehead so you won't forget? Judson 6-2100.

And now, on with the old-fashioned revival hour.

We have a phone flickering here. But everytime I pick it up the light goes off. Oh, there's somebody here.

Hello! Who is this? . . . Harvey Maguire? . . . On *What's My Line?* tonight you say I guessed that a man was an undertaker and you're calling me to tell me that you are an undertaker too? Well, that's nice to know because we all have to go sometime. Have you ever been on *What's My Line?* . . . You tried but you didn't get on? Well, actually, on quiz programs these days, Harvey, undertakers are kind of a drug on the market. . . . Could you possibly become a Gloucester deep-sea fisherman for about four weeks? I think I could sneak you in. . . . You tried that? . . . Now you're an undertaker. For fish? . . . You want to know what my television plans are? Well, at the moment I plan to continue the payments on my set. . . . Well, Harvey, thanks a million for calling tonight. Bye.

III

All sorts of notes are coming in now. America's favorite troubadour is here. Do you know who America's favorite troubadour is?

MAN: No.

ALLEN: That's what I like about you. You agree with everything. America's favorite troubadour is Tom Scott, the eminent composer and balladeer. Tom is the fellow who did the music for *Robin Hood*. Did you see *Robin Hood?*

MAN: No.

ALLEN: You're turning into a mystery man. What is your name, in case your mother is listening?

MAN: Shall I tell you?

ALLEN: It's up to you. Do you want to?

DWAR: I don't care. My name is Richard Dwar.

ALLEN: Nice to have you here, Mr. Dwar. And what are the names of some of the other folks in your party?

DWAR: *Mrs.* Dwar.

ALLEN: All three of them? Well, more power to you.

We promised you folks that Jim Moran would be up after the news. And I don't think it will do him much good to come up after the news because I won't give it to him. But let's get him up right now. Here he is, a fellow who has pulled off more crazy stunts than you could shake a stick at and it's very difficult to shake a stick at a crazy stunt. Here's Jim Moran.

MORAN: How are you?

ALLEN: Fine. Jim is smoking the tiniest pipe. Is that

a pipe or a tear duct? That pipe is the smallest thing hanging off a face I ever saw in my life.

MORAN: The smaller the pipe, the more sensitive.

ALLEN: That will be our thought for the day.

MORAN: Okay. You'd better give me a thought because I don't have any.

ALLEN: Where did you get that pipe?

MORAN: This was given to me by John Kaljikan. He's an export-import man having to do with things in Tangiers, the money exchange. And he transfers *piastras* to *rials*.

ALLEN: Watch your language!

MORAN: To *lira* to—

ALLEN: Bing Crosby did that very well. Toora-lira-lira—

MORAN: To *pesos*. Every time I go down there everybody says you take your *rials* and I'll give you 350 for twenty. And so I give it to the man—

ALLEN: Steady!

MORAN: And then I get the *rials*. Now, he says, I'll tell you what I'm going to do.

ALLEN: Fight it, Jim.

MORAN: I'm going to get you 350 *piastras* for this, so I get the 350 *piastras*. I end up with less money. John Kaljikan can go down there and he always ends up with *more* money. . . . He bought me this small pipe, by the way.

ALLEN: I don't think it's *you*, Jim.

MORAN: Let's face it. I'm a real nut, otherwise I would not even be here.

ALLEN: We're both in the same boat.

MORAN: No, you're doing great things now. Is it not

true that you have replaced George Kaufman on *This Is Show Business?* And is it not true that you have replaced Hal Bloch on *What's My Line?*

ALLEN: I'm afraid it is.

MORAN: I want to tell you something, Steve. I've been depressed by television. But I feel that television shows its wisdom in putting you in. I'm not kidding. Stand up and take a bow. Steve Allen, ladies and gentlemen.

ALLEN: Jim, you sober old son-of-a-gun, it's nice to have you in the house. Actually, George Kaufman will be back, I'm happy to say, two weeks from tonight. I've been busy the last week, myself, writing a new lyric to "Silent Night."*

MORAN: You know, you are a fast person with a quip whereas I am more of a relaxed, peaceable, and friendly type of person.

ALLEN: All right, Jim, lie down.

MORAN: And so I don't want you to give me this japery and fast talk because I'm too slow to catch it. When I *listen* to it I think it's great. But when I'm up here I think it's pretty horrible for you to do it to me.

ALLEN: Jim, that isn't japery, and I'm no Jackanapes. Where did you get the cigars, Jim? Did you buy them or did somebody have a baby?

MORAN: I'm going to smoke one of those now if it's all right with you.

ALLEN: It isn't, but go ahead.

MORAN: I purchased them in the *foyer*. Is that the way you pronounce it?

ALLEN: No, but you're entitled to your opinion.

* Kaufman had just been taken off *This Is Show Business* for making a derogatory reference to "Silent Night."

MORAN: It's not an opinion. It's a statement.

ALLEN: Oh, I thought you said "fooey." You said foyer. Say, that's a *long* cigar. Watch it, Jim. If you light it the whole building will go up.

MORAN: I have to bite it first.

ALLEN: He doesn't smoke them, he just bites them. Oh, he *does* smoke them. The waiters in this neighborhood are very nice. A waiter just came up, from another restaurant, and lit this cigar.

MORAN: Now I want to tell you something about cigar smoking. There are dealers who take a fat cigar and put it in their fat face and they chew most of the day and they make deals. Now I'm a *veranda* smoker, a man who sits back on a small porch with big columns four stories high. And I take a draw on this cigar and look out over the hounds and horses and the rolling hills of Virginia and I count my blessings.

ALLEN: You're a blessing counter.

MORAN: Yes. Notice the way a veranda smoker smokes. You do not clench the cigar in your teeth.

ALLEN: What do you do, stick it in your ear?

MORAN: No. Every now and then you draw on it, with great reverence. You close your eyes and you get a sweet look on your face when you draw on the fine, long cigar and look over your acres.

ALLEN: Jim, where the hell have you *been* tonight?

MORAN: Well, I had a most beautiful dinner, cooked by one of the finest cooks in the whole world, by the name of Merle Armitidge. Have you ever heard of him?

ALLEN: [*Incredulously*] Have I ever heard of Merle Armitidge? [*Pause*] *No.* What does he do?

MORAN: Right now he is the art director of *Look*

magazine, but prior to that he was one of the greatest entrepreneurs that this country has ever had. He has brought some of the finest talent to this country. He is partly responsible for the Hollywood Bowl.

ALLEN: And I can imagine how tough it was bringing the Hollywood Bowl to this country.

MORAN: Now he's a cook. He wrote a book called *Fit for a King*. And it's one of the finest cookbooks that's ever been written.

ALLEN: Was that Merle who just stood up on the table and shouted?

MORAN: No, Merle Armitidge is a man I have an enormous regard for. This man cooked a meal tonight that—well, the only salt that was in this meal was the salt that came from the tears in my eyes that fell into the soup.

ALLEN: Jim, that's the loveliest thing I've ever heard. Don't ever say anything like it again. But I know you've written very dramatic advertising prose. Have you ever tried your hand at poetry?

MORAN: No. I write children's books.

ALLEN: Really? Tell us about these children's books, Jim. Jim, put the beer down and tell us about the children's books.

MORAN: I don't want you to rush me, Steve, because you know . . .

ALLEN: I know. You're on your veranda.

MORAN: I have one of them in my zither case in the anteroom there.

ALLEN: A veranda in your zither case? Oh, a *book!* Did you say zither case?

MORAN: Yes, I play the zither. I gave a zither concert tonight for the assembled guests of Merle Armitidge.

ALLEN: How large is your zither?

MORAN: Thirty-eight strings.

ALLEN: Don't you have a tendency to run out of fingers?

MORAN: No, no. It has to do with *deftness*.

ALLEN: Oh, I can *hear* you pretty well.

MORAN: I sure walked right into that one. You shouldn't do that to me, Steve.

ALLEN: I'll take anything I can get. Do I want to sound literate up here? I've got to sound stupid because that's where the laughs are. Is your zither over there? Would you favor us with a number?

MORAN: Well, I shouldn't play here, on account of the union. If you wish me to, I'll play, but it's against the law.

ALLEN: I don't know . . . I was down at the union the other day, and *they* can't play either. They're politicians, not musicians.

MORAN: Anyway, I said that my script for my latest children's book was in my guitar case. *Zither* case, rather.

ALLEN: All right, then play your cigar for all I care. Where is the zither? I mean, get the child out of that case.

MORAN: I honestly do not know whether it's legal or not. I think this could throw you in jail.

ALLEN: Are you a member of the musicians' union?

MORAN: No, I'm not.

ALLEN: Then you can play.

MORAN: I'm *not*, then I can play?

ALLEN: It's ridiculous, but it's true.

MORAN: All right. Bring me the case.

ALLEN: May we have the zither case, please? There goes a man. I hope he's going for the zither. If he comes back it will be a good sign.

MORAN: I need a footstool. Something the size of three telephone directories.

ALLEN: I'm sorry, you can't make any outside calls.

MORAN: I'm not going to just play.

ALLEN: But we've been counting on it. Here comes a small case. That's a *guitar* case.

MORAN: Well, I'll play the guitar, if they can't find the zither.

ALLEN: You can play the *case* as far as I'm concerned. Jim, that doesn't look like a zither to me. But then, what does?

[*Moran strokes the strings and Allen sings*]

ALLEN: "Do not forsake me, oh my darlin'." You don't mind if I sing with you, do you, Jim? But I had no idea you were musically inclined. And boy, was I right! No, that's a very fine instrument. Where did you pick this up? It looks like it's made out of an old cigar box.

MORAN: May I tune this down to an A, please?

ALLEN: You want to *tune* it?

[*Moran tunes the zither and plays*]

ALLEN: That's lovely. It really is. And here come the lawyers from Local 807.

MORAN: Seven bars is a violation.

ALLEN: How many did you stop at on your way over here?

MORAN: I haven't sung anything yet. I'm going to do just two bars.

ALLEN: These are very long bars. This is a nine-beat bar we're working with tonight. I can make my own rules.

MORAN: Would you mind, old man? I'm playing.

[*Moran plays the zither and hums softly*]

ALLEN: Go to sleep, everyone. That's six and a half bars and it's very pretty.

And so another evensong serenade comes to a close. It's been the sweet strings of Jim Moran and his synphonette brought to you by people who wear long jeans and old sweat shirts. Jim, you did yourself proud there. That's an old expression, and you've got an old expression yourself.

MORAN: And many are called but few are chosen. You know that, Steve, and you're one of those.

ALLEN: Well, give me a call and we'll choose somebody some night, Jim. What are you working on now? Are you still promoting Persian rugs?

MORAN: No, I'm *thinking*. This is why I can't speak much tonight. Now, Steve, you look at me with that eye. I see that you're perpetrating something. You're not listening to me. You're waiting so that you can make a joke out of anything I say.

ALLEN: No, that's not the secret. The secret of talking to people is to listen carefully to *everything* they say because they are walking straight lines. It sounds cruel, but if I *didn't* listen to you I'd be in a heck of a spot.

MORAN: Hey, I should have had that zither up here because I need a resonant table. And this looks like a resonant table. The zither has three prongs that dig into the wood.

ALLEN: That sounds like the name of a good trio. Here they are friends, "The Three Prongs," digging into the wood once again. You mean you can play this either in your arms, cradled gently guitar-style, or lying flat on a table?

MORAN: No, this method is for the guitar. My instrument is a zither. This is why I have so many calluses on my hand. Look at those calluses. What do you think they're from?

ALLEN: Hunger. Those are the *smallest* calluses.

MORAN: Sometimes you really make me quite depressed. But I have such an effervescence in my heart that I'm going to rise above you, old man.

ALLEN: I *noticed* you were floating around a bit. Say, listen, that's a very fancy waistcoat you're wearing.

MORAN: Thank you.

ALLEN: Jim is impeccably dressed tonight. He's wearing a black suit and a sort of a tattersall waistcoat, and a tie that's all tattered too. And a nice black tie with a pearl stickpin which is causing him to bleed slightly because the pin is stuck in his chest bone. That's a nice little pearl stickpin. You are the epitome of good taste tonight.

MORAN: Well, it's not my idea of what a person would do if he were trying to fool somebody.

ALLEN: Why are you trying to confuse?

MORAN: I'm not trying to confuse anyone. Now look at you, for example. I understood there was a man who walked up Madison Avenue three days ago that actually had a *double*-breasted suit on.

ALLEN: You mean I'm in uniform.

MORAN: You look like what they're *supposed* to look like. You are a person who has conformed to the taskmasters that employ you. Now I would not do that. They

would look at me and they would know that *I* was one
of the taskmasters.

ALLEN: A very sound way to look at it, Jim.

MORAN: Whereas you have conformed. Let me see
your shoes. See? You've got everything on that everybody is supposed to have on on Madison Avenue. Look at
the big cuff links, four buttons on the sleeves, three buttons on the front. Single-breasted, television shirt. They
have *had* you. They are using you, Steve. You are bigger
than this. I'm telling you, drop these people. Get out of
it.

ALLEN: Jim, if it will make you any happier—

MORAN: You haven't even got the handkerchief in
there.

ALLEN: I know. The waiters have light fingers. Jim,
if it will make you happy I'll do the rest of the show in
my underwear. Though I admit I'm wearing Brooks
Brothers Oxford buttoned-down underwear.

MORAN: Give me the name of your shoemaker.

ALLEN: Charlie.

MORAN: Okay. I notice you have long socks on. Why
is that?

ALLEN: Because I have long legs.

MORAN: A lot of people have these short California-
type socks.

ALLEN: They've got short California-type legs. These
people are wrong thinkers from the word go, and I may
say the word.

MORAN: Stand up, Steve, and turn around, and let me
look at you, will you please?

ALLEN: To tell you the truth I can't stand up on
this little platform, because I'm very tall.

MORAN: Oh, I see.

ALLEN: And this is a low-budget program.

MORAN: Well, is it all right if I smoke my veranda cigar?

ALLEN: Jim, it's all right with me if you burn the building down.

MORAN: Are there any questions?

ALLEN: Are there any answers?

MORAN: Yes, I've got answers. Do you want to pick a subject? Pick a subject.

ALLEN: Bring me my subject-pick, please.

MORAN: I came up here with nothing to talk about.

ALLEN: And that's the way it's been going.

MORAN: And you got me so damned involved in cigars, verandas, and Virginia.

ALLEN: Jim, I'll tell you what we'll do here. We'll make a buck or two for the station. I want you to stay but I just want to take a peck at a commercial I have to do for the Auto Van and Warehouse Corporation. You all know about them, of course. So it's hardly worthwhile my telling you. The Auto Van and Warehouse Corporation, operated by Fisher and Brothers at 438 West Fifty-first Street, is tops in the field of office, loft, and home removals. If you'd like to have your loft removed get down there and they'll do it.

They have courteous, efficient personnel and the most up-to-date equipment. They service your needs, from start to finish, and whether you're moving around the corner (and remember, when you're on the corner always keep moving) call Fisher and Brothers for an estimate. And they'll estimate that you've called them. For the tops in moving, storage, packing, and crating call Fisher and Brothers. And now, Jim.

MORAN: I want to talk about the Bunny Hop.

ALLEN: Now you're getting sensible.

MORAN: Well, I *do* want to talk about the Bunny Hop.

ALLEN: Have you ever done it?

MORAN: Yes, I did it the other day. I was caught in a Bunny Hop line in the Capitol Theatre, and my cubic displacement is such as to make it quite difficult.

ALLEN: What is a seven-liter boat?

MORAN: Anyway, every four bars you have to hop three times and I hopped three times on every four bars and that is why I was late getting here.

ALLEN: Well, as long as you didn't hop *seven* bars we won't have to pay you so that's all right. Where are you going after you leave?

MORAN: Are you now inquiring about my departure?

ALLEN: I am, but with no ulterior motive. I don't *want* you to leave, but I'll worry about you when you do.

MORAN: When you say something like that I feel that you wish me to depart.

ALLEN: Jim, that's not the truth. I could get a cheap laugh and say yes, but I really want you to stick around.

MORAN: All right, I'm sticking around. What do you want me to talk about though?

ALLEN: Somebody sent up a card a while ago and they wanted to know if people who slyly plug products on the radio get anything in return for it.

MORAN: I think that anyone who would sit at an open microphone and plug anything commercial for un- der the table dollars is a person that has been had. I don't think they should do it. I like to think that children are growing up in a wholesome world and I would not like them to know about these things. How much money have you got?

ALLEN: Jim, there are two sides to every story. There was a fellow who used to write for me. I replaced Eve Arden on radio during the summer and—

MORAN: You played Eve Arden?

ALLEN: I *replaced* Eve Arden. There's a straight line, too, but we'll leave it alone. And a fellow wrote a joke for me about—

MORAN: You've got people that write—you don't make your own jokes?

ALLEN: On *that* kind of a program I have writers.

MORAN: This is a horrible thing for me to think, that a person as fast and as witty as you would hire some hireling, as Shakespeare said, to write a quip for you. You did this?

ALLEN: Yes, I hired a fellow named Ling. He was a Chinese gag writer, for fortune cookies. So much for hirelings. On some programs I ad-lib, like this, but I find that it makes actors nervous if they're reading and you're ad-libbing. They get panicky and they complain to the union, so we do have writers on other shows.

Anyway, this fellow wrote a joke for me about a Bendix. For thirteen weeks—the program was on that long—he wrote a joke every week about a Bendix washing machine. And, would you believe it, at the end of the summer four trucks pulled up front of that man's house out in Van Nuys, California, and unloaded on his lawn thirteen Bendix washing machines. He is now out of radio altogether. He's running a laundromat and it just goes to show you that sometimes out of the darkness can come light, if you know what I mean, and I don't.

Jim, where did you buy that suit?

MORAN: This is not a suit. No, I feel that if a person goes out in the night he should be dressed—

ALLEN: I think that's an admirable idea. Jim, where *did* you get that suit? It's a black suit and it's a very unusual material. It looks like a cut-down submarine uniform.

MORAN: This is British twill.

ALLEN: Well, I suppose 'twill, but where did you get it?

MORAN: I'll tell you something about the way *you* are dressed. You have your sleeves pressed. And this is not allowed on Madison Avenue.

ALLEN: That's my one gesture of defiance.

MORAN: This used to be the thing you could do. But not now. You notice that there's no crease in *my* sleeves.

ALLEN: Actually, my *sleeves* are all right. I happen to have a crease in my *arm*.

Well, Jim, you've been here tonight—

MORAN: You wish me to depart? Is this true or not?

ALLEN: To tell you the truth—

MORAN: When anybody says, "Come back again, love to see you, any time you're in town," this never happens. Nobody ever comes back again, on any shows. Is it not right?

ALLEN: Yes. And it's not right.

MORAN: Now, do you wish me to stay or do you wish me to go?

ALLEN: I wish you to come back again. And you know

that I'm the one person when I say it I mean it because I've said that to you before and you're here.

MORAN: Okay. But now you wish me to depart.

ALLEN: To tell you the truth, Jim, it's a negative thing. *I* don't wish you to go. But you *have* to, because—

MORAN: I *have* to go?

ALLEN: Isn't that blunt of me?

MORAN: You're asking me to . . . ?

ALLEN: I'm *telling you,* Jim. I want to lay it right on the line. No, what I was getting at, Jim—there are a few *other* people here. And we've got fourteen commercials we're behind here. Let me see.

Milady's Blintzes. What the heck is that? I'll figure this out and then I'll let you in on it. Milady's Blintzes have proven I-T-A. Yes? Oh, then it goes on to explain. Yes, Milady's has I-T-A and that means "International-Taste-Appeal." Well, they lost me already. However, the things probably taste swell and that's what they're trying to tell you in their own shy way. When you want to be *sure* ask for Milady's Blintzes. If she's hungry, she won't *give* them to you, but that's the chance you have to take. You can laugh, but one night here I asked for the Chef's Special and the guy says, "I'm sorry you can't have it. The chef is still eating it."

What does it say here now? They're so simple and easy to serve. Just take them out of the freezer and brown and serve. You remember them. Great dance team. Brown and Serve. Heat and Eat. They were good, too. Your taste buds will get an additional threat—I mean *treat*—with the five delicious fillings, strawberry with cheese, cheese with strawberry, blueberry, cherry, potato, and you-should-live-so-long. Get Milady's—I'll spell that for you—T-H-A-T.

Milady's products are available at all stores carrying frozen foods, and don't *you* try to carry frozen foods or you'll burn your hands off. Try them and you'll see why Milady's Blintzes are an international favorite. Do it today because they're chockful of downright goodness. It doesn't say that, but I think it should. Remember the days when *all* commercials ended up with *chockful of downright goodness?* So put it in your crankcase today. Marfak! Chockful of downright goodness.

IV

Bob Carroll is here, and then, of course, Jim Moran is still here. Jim is very happy tonight because he's celebrating his forty-third birthday. Passed out cold under his table. Let's get Bob Carroll up here. Ladies and gentlemen, one of the brightest young baritones in the business. Bob Carroll. How are you doing, Bob?

CARROLL: All right, Steve.

ALLEN: Bob, I understand you have a new recording which is making great strides in disc-jockey circles around the country. What's the name of it?

CARROLL: Well, Steve, it's called, "Say It with Your Heart," and it's making great strides in disc-jockey . . .

Steve Nelson, who also wrote a song that I can't remember—something about—it wasn't "Rudolph, the Red-nosed Reindeer." It was some other big kid's song like "Go to Sleep, You Little Rat," something like that.

ALLEN: Isn't he also the fellow who wrote one of my favorite songs called "The Moon Was Yellow, and I

Was Pretty Chicken Myself." Bob, where are you staying now?

CARROLL: Well, Steve, I'm living with you.

ALLEN: So that was you I heard last night. No, actually, Bob *is* rooming with me. And you *were* very noisy last night. I heard you coming home. And he came in the *window*. Which isn't too easy because I live on the twenty-fourth floor.

CARROLL: By the way, Steve, I don't mind working for my keep, but when you ask me to hammer nails in the wall to put mirrors up I object to the dents in my bare hands. A hammer would help.

ALLEN: It was a rather unusual assignment. As I recall, I asked you to put a mirror on the ceiling of my bathroom so I could watch myself gargle. Is that right?

CARROLL: That's true.

ALLEN: All right, I tell you what we'll do right now, Bob.

CARROLL: What, Steve?

ALLEN: We'll go home. No, we'll play your record, and then while *that's* on we'll go home. What's the label, by the way?

CARROLL: It's the Derby label.

ALLEN: That's right. This record is available in two sizes, seventy-eight and six and seven-eighths. It's a Derby record. You can either play it or wear it. "Say It with Your Nose."

[*Record is played*]

ALLEN: Bob, I understand you're going to open at the Chicago Theatre in a week or two. Who is on the bill with you?

CARROLL: Dave Barry. Dave and I will be on the bill

along with a third-dimensional film. It's the picture that you see when you wear the dark glasses, and it comes out third-dimensional.

ALLEN: I remember I saw a picture like that a few years ago and I wore one big green cellophane glass and one big red cellophane glass and several people picked up my head. They thought I had it wrapped for Christmas.

What does this note say? Can you read this?

CARROLL: Mr. and Mrs. Hy Grund. That's legit. Mr. and Mrs. Hy Grund of Middletown, Ohio, attending the metals convention.

ALLEN: Are you Hy Grund? Would you mind moving to even higher ground so I can see you a little better? Ohio, that's the heart of the bird belt over there.

CARROLL: Sure it is. They've got a lot of steel birds flying around there.

Say, you've got a tan.

ALLEN: I've been using a sun lamp lately. I've been using a Spurty sun lamp.

CARROLL: A Spurty sun lamp?

ALLEN: Yes.

CARROLL: Get any on you?

ALLEN: It spurted all over me. That's right, Bob, burned my nose off. But seriously, it's given me a little color. Which is wonderful if you like blue.

CARROLL: Steve, may I ask you something?

ALLEN: Anything, Bob.

CARROLL: Rather personal?

ALLEN: No.

CARROLL: I'd like to find out a little more about this show you're going to do on ABC.

ALLEN: It will feature entirely service talent, fellows

in the Air Force and in the Army. It has a rather long title. The full title of the show is *The United States Army and Air Force Talent Patrol*. This takes up the first twelve minutes of the program. Then there's three minutes of entertainment and then they work the title in again and that fills in the half hour.

CARROLL: Who are you splitting billing with—General Van Fleet? Seriously, Steve, do you go to army bases around New York or do you do the show right from the studio?

ALLEN: No, the Army comes to me . . . and shoots the heck out of me.

CARROLL: How do you find the talent?

ALLEN: Pretty good. No, they send a man out, a talent scout who goes all over the world. We pay all their expenses and give them a nice time while they're here and then they get some fine prizes. If you win on the program, you get an honorable discharge, I think. And if you lose . . .

CARROLL: You stay in. What kind of musical backing will you have on the show?

ALLEN: They're going to have the West Point Band and then on alternate weeks one of the Air Force bands. Mitchell Field—Marshall Field, I don't know, *some* field is going to send over a bunch of fellows and try to get instruments for each man, so send in your egg whites and we'll convert them into stamps for those orphans.

CARROLL: I think you make sense, Steve.

ALLEN: The talent is going to be very good. In format it will be like *Talent Scouts* with khaki tea bags.

CARROLL: Khaki tea bags! Well, Steve I wish you a lot of luck on it. You've got your sponsor, haven't you?

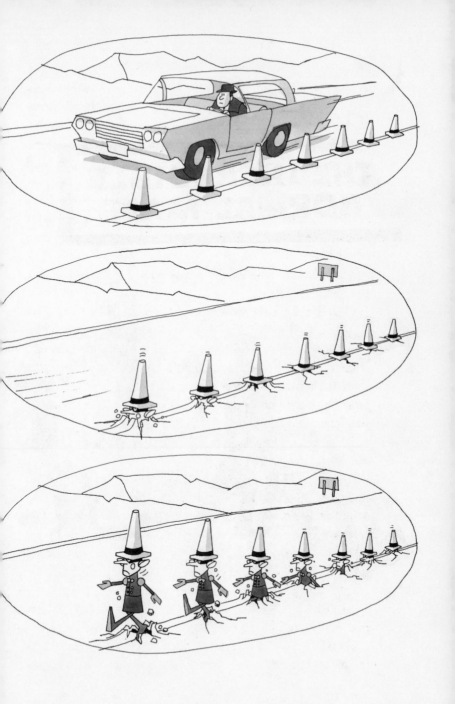

ALLEN: Yes, Uncle Sam.

CARROLL: If, say, Armco steel wanted to pick up the tab for fifteen minutes of the show, would it be impossible for them to do so?

ALLEN: No, the government is quite willing to share the expense with private enterprise, which is probably the first time in the history of the nation this has occurred. But it actually will be available to sponsorship. If even some foreign government would like to buy fifteen minutes we'll be glad to do a commercial in any language, and we could probably do a very fine job for the French Foreign Legion. Does that answer your question, and what was it, by the way?

CARROLL: I forgot. But I'm very glad that you're now taking over the Siamese talent hour.

Well, Steve.

ALLEN: Yes, Bob?

CARROLL: Well, Steve.

ALLEN: Yes, Bob?

CARROLL: These are the moments that touch me.

ALLEN: These are the times that try men's souls. Would you like to try mine for size? I'm getting tired of it. Hey, speaking of souls, I want to show you something. See these socks? Aren't they nice? They're genuine nylon rib with a cellophane heel. I got these when I was out on the coast last week at a wonderful place out there— Western Auto stores. Twenty-nine cents for these socks, twenty-nine cents. They had a big sale. I'm telling you, no more of those thirty-one-cent socks for me.

CARROLL: Steve, I admire your courage because I'm very cheap too. You see the socks I've got on? This is legit. Those of you who want to go shopping and impress everybody by making it over to Brooks Brothers, I wish you luck. But, you see, with people like you and me, we glorified gypsies who travel . . . well, you *don't* travel, you're on television.

ALLEN: No, but I glorify gypsies.

Where *did* you pick those socks up, Bob? And how soon are you going to put them down?

CARROLL: I bought these in a very exclusive town, Miami Beach, Florida. I refuse to be caught up in the whirl of expensive living that goes on down there.

ALLEN: There's nothing wrong at *all* with navy surplus socks. They're perfectly okay.

CARROLL: Well, see this suit?

ALLEN: Not quite, it's a little smoky in here.

CARROLL: That's because most of it has been worn off.

ALLEN: But it's coming through now. Yes, there it is!

CARROLL: This is a very cheap suit.

ALLEN: You folks should have seen it before the battery wore down. No, it's a lovely suit. Where did you get it?

CARROLL: I got this one from Jim Moran because I subscribe to his theory of living. But I don't believe in those expensive argyle socks. Laundries get hold of them on the road, you know, and they come back looking like Napoleon's battle flags.

ALLEN: I don't know, if they wear out you can always stitch two of them together and play checkers.

CARROLL: You don't want to buy the last fifteen minutes of Steve's new show, do you, sir? [*Pause*] He sits there and blandly says no. Would you mind leaving?

ALLEN: No, that's Harry Bland, and I don't want you to insult him.

CARROLL: As a matter of fact, sir, I hope someday that you will pick up the tab for a show that Steve and I may get fired from.

ALLEN: I'll be doing all right if he picks up the tab at his table tonight. Say, there's a phone call, Bob. Go ahead. Say there's a phone call, Bob.

CARROLL: There's a phone call, Bob.

ALLEN: Thanks, Bob. Hello, Men's Summer Home. Some are in and some are out. . . . What? You've been listening to Barry Gray? You have very good ears! You'd like to say that you're disappointed because Barry announced I was going to have a talent program for *amateur* talent? Well, I'll tell you. Some of the talent that we use on the program *will* be amateur talent, although it will be *service* talent. I don't know what you play but if you can manage to get yourself drafted in about four weeks I'll mention your name. . . . Oh, you sing and write songs? You see, I'm repeating what you say. So say something. . . . You don't know the first thing about getting a job in television? Or getting a song published? Actually it's very tough.

You can say a lot of encouraging things to amateur songwriters but there's one discouraging fact they should face, not so they should be discouraged and kill themselves but because you should apprise yourself of all the facts involved.

There are probably a million people in this nation, literally, who can write a fair song, at least one fair song. But there's only a market for about four hundred songs a year. So arithmetic is against you.

Naturally, amateurs do break into the field every year, but only about five or six of them. I think there are more people than that hit by lightning every year in this country. So why don't you collaborate with a lightning bolt?

Have you written any other novelties? Actually, publishers are more interested in novelties than they are in ballads. . . . You've written novelties and ballads? . . . You must have tried it with at least fifty friends? The song, you mean? . . . Good. Mary, I wish you lots of good luck. I have several other calls coming in. From waiters. Nice to talk to you, Mary. Good night.

Oh, we have to do a few commercials. Bob, have you ever slept on a Sealy mattress?

CARROLL: Have I ever slept on a Sealy mattress?

ALLEN: I asked you first.

CARROLL: I probably have, Steve.

ALLEN: If it's a Sealy it can easily happen. Isn't that heartwarming? It's a chockful of downright feathers.

And it's a must on your back. [*Commercial*]

V

Now let's get Tom Scott up here. Hi, Tom, nice to see you. We announced earlier this evening that you did the music for *Robin Hood*. Does that mean you wrote the score for the picture?

SCOTT: Steve, I don't feel like talking tonight. But since you've done me this honor, I will nevertheless attempt to rise above my laryngitis. And I've had a little Old Grandad.

ALLEN: That's all right. My old grandad was kind of small himself.

SCOTT: Now you asked me a direct question.

ALLEN: And that's the last one you'll get because you gave me a very evasive answer. No, did you write the music, Tom, for *Robin Hood?*

SCOTT: Yes. I'm a composer, Steve. And it's an awfully hard life.

ALLEN: Sure, because there are one million people who can write songs and only three people who can read egg whites, so where does that leave the amateur songwriter, and you spilled a little beer. Tom, do you record?

SCOTT: Yes.

ALLEN: For what label? [*Scott belches*] Oh, really?

SCOTT: Coral. Do you want to hear one of the songs?

ALLEN: Can you hum it?

[*Scott starts humming but in a very low key*]

SCOTT: I'm a little low, I think.

ALLEN: I don't think you're low. I think you're high.

SCOTT: May I say before we go any further, Steve, I think you're one of the fastest ad-libbers, fast talkers, et cetera, people . . . honestly. You have done a noble job. I mean, you've sat here and the words have flowed out from you like western cattle coming out of the corral.

ALLEN: You mean it's all been a lot of bull.

SCOTT: But, now look here, Steve, you asked me to sing and you're trying to evade that. You're another one of these Yankees. So clever, so subtle, and you come down and take over our noble Southland.

ALLEN: Where are you from?

SCOTT: I'm from Kentucky, God bless her.

ALLEN: Now I know where that veranda is located.

SCOTT: Steve, do you know that Kentucky is only seven hundred miles from here?

78 BIGGER THAN A BREADBOX

ALLEN: Well, we're off the air in an hour.

SCOTT: Yes, we've got everything there. We've got mountains. We've got rivers, valleys, wonderful bourbon whiskey.

ALLEN: I take it you just got in.

SCOTT: You know, you asked me to sing and you're just being clever. You don't *want* to hear me sing, do you?

ALLEN: I don't think you're going to give yourself a chance, but I'd love to hear you.

SCOTT: Did I tell you about my new album? It's released by Coral Records, who are remotely, in some strange mysterious way in which only Wall Street brokers know about, connected with Decca. I don't know what the connection is, but they have the same offices.

ALLEN: The only difference between the two firms is Coral doesn't pay rent.

SCOTT: Only a Yankee would have observed that.

ALLEN: I've just been handed a note by the legal adviser and he says that it's all right as long as you sing only seven bars, Tom.

SCOTT: Well, he's wrong. My father was a lawyer and my father's pappy was a lawyer and I know more about the copyrights of these United States than either my father or his pappy knew. And I happen to know that it's perfectly legal for me to sing anything, including "The Star-Spangled Banner," provided I do not have a musical accompaniment.

You just need somebody who's an authority to say that it's all right to do it. Now, who can be a better authority than me? I come from Kentucky.

ALLEN: To tell you the truth it isn't the copyright

problem that they're worried about. I think it's the fact that as a regular member of the *union*—if you'll pardon the expression—you might have to be paid for singing, not that the writers will have to be paid for the use of their material.

SCOTT: Those Yankees! They never want to pay for it, do they?

ALLEN: It isn't that so much. It's that tonight *I'd* have to pay for it.

SCOTT: You know the best way to get out of this?

ALLEN: Yes. Sing seven bars, and then stop, and then sing seven other bars. Skip every eighth bar.

SCOTT: No. Here's the way out. Since we cannot sing let us recite. You have spoken of poetry. I'm a student of poetry. It's sort of a hobby of mine. And I want to say to you, Steve, and to the people assembled here, and to all of these United States and anybody else who, by short wave or remote control or by being backed off the far planets and those little waves bouncing back down, might hear us—wherever, be it a kiosk in Karamajunior, perhaps—that the folk songs of America have the richest and deepest poetry of any that I've ever read and that some of those folk songs will be found in my new album called "Sing of America."

ALLEN: God bless us, everyone!

I think it's wonderful, Tom, that you're interested in folk music, because there are an awful lot of *folks*, you know?

SCOTT: Now, seriously, I used to have an alcoholic friend—

ALLEN: Well, to each his own.

SCOTT: This man had a strange problem. He had to

drink whiskey once in a while, and he *hated* whiskey. I mean the mere sight of a bottle would cause this man to turn pale and run.

ALLEN: I ran for a pail once myself, but go ahead.

SCOTT: He just hated it. But he *had* to drink it. And we tried various ways, since he had to, to get it down. It was like medicine, you know, like sustenance to him. Without it he'd simply collapse.

ALLEN: Good for him.

SCOTT: A pale, palpitating heap on the floor. So we tried various methods and we found, oddly enough, that the only way we could get it down him was to *recite*. I went through all the poetry that I knew. I began with "Let me not to the marriage of true minds, admit impediments"; "Love is not love, which alters when it alteration finds or bends with the remover to remove. Oh, no! It is an ever fixed mark which looks on tempests but is not shaken." We tried that. Couldn't even get a dram of *gin* near his face. Then I tried those immortal words "Hail, bright plane." That didn't work either.

And we thought and we thought. And finally it was in the folk songs, lines like "Where do you come from? Where do you go? Where do you come from, my cotton-eyed Joe? Come for to see you, Come for to sing, Come for to show you my diamond ring." Well, I had no more got that out than this man had consumed a whole quart of Old Grandad.

From that time on I knew this was the easiest way to get whiskey down a man who had to have whiskey. Mind you, I'm not saying that a man *should* or shouldn't. This was his problem. We reversed it. We cured him. We healed him. A very good, solid, and stable citizen. Last I saw of him he was coming out of the Chase National Bank.

ALLEN: Walking backward with a gun in his hand I presume.

A lot of people come out of banks, Tom, but it's what happened *inside* that really counts. Well, Tom, you've been very *sotto voce* tonight. And I want to thank you for it because if they'd ever really heard you we'd be dead. Really, it was very nice of you to come up.

SCOTT: Can I stay a little longer?

ALLEN: Sure.

SCOTT: Can I say a little poetry for you?

ALLEN: Sure, you can, and I'll recite some for you.

SCOTT: Good! You know the lines that begin "Western Wind, when wilt thou blow, That the small rain down may rain?" Do you? "O gentle death when wilt thou come, And I to my love am calling in vain." Or do you ever sing rounds?

ALLEN: Once in a while.

SCOTT: Is it legal to sing a round?

ALLEN: It depends where you're singing around, I guess. It's not legal to sing around here.

SCOTT: I think it would be an awful lot of fun. It has never been done in this restaurant before and it's perfectly legal. But none of the rounds run more than four bars and since seven bars is the limit I think the whole restaurant should join with us and sing a good old Christmas round.

ALLEN: This could last a few weeks. But let's do sing a Christmas round because it's been a very round Christmas.

SCOTT: All right. Do you know the one that begins "My dame has a lame tame crane?"

ALLEN: What else have you got? Be with you in a minute, Tom. First I have to ruin a little commercial here.

Friends, if you're tossing around in bed unable to sleep because of a lumpy, bumpy mattress what you need is a Sealy posturepedic mattress. Slipping on a Sealy—slipping on the ceiling—is like sloping on a thing. It's more relaxing. It's firmer, and you're sleeping anyway so don't fight it.

Scientifically made to give extra support to your vital third. (I didn't even know I *had* one.) Sealy posturepedic innerspring is, *one,* approved for advertising by the *American Medical Association Journal.* And anyone who would associate with the *American Medical Journal should* go to sleep.

Two, it's been granted the *Good Housekeeping* approval of seals, by the program *Zoo Parade. Three,* it's commended by *Parents' Magazine.* In fact, I don't know of a better way to become a parent. And, *four,* it's approved by *Today's Health.* And *five,* I forget. So remember those five reasons and I'll see you later.

It's guaranteed for ten full years, unless you sleep on it . . . and it's on sale at leading department stores where you'll also find the famous Sealy Posturepedic mattress recommended for children.

Tested and approved for growing young bodies. Have you ever grown a young body? Don't answer that. Or write to me at White Sands proving grounds.

Tom . . .

SCOTT: Yes, Steve?

ALLEN: It seems like only yesterday . . . and I think

it was. I'd like you to come on some night and bring your guitar.

SCOTT: I'd love to. Do you know "The Colorado Trail?"

ALLEN: Know it? I roomed on it for about eight weeks.

SCOTT: Do you want to hear just a little of that? It's got a beautiful tune. If you want to hear it listen to my album "Sing of America," et cetera, et cetera, et cetera.

ALLEN: Okay, Tom. Thanks for coming up. Tom Scott, America's favorite troubadour. I have another little commercial for you. For Kolmer-Marcus. It says here, ad-lib from copy points below. It's been a long time since I've ad-libbed so I may have a little trouble with it.

Number One. It's Kolmer-Marcus's semiannual clearance of suits, top coats, overcoats, sports jackets, and slacks, plus a special group of tuxedos. *Point Two.* This large selection of traditionally fine clothing is from Kolmer-Marcus's regular stock. I don't know who gets the *other stuff*, but you have to be satisfied with the regular stock. Incidentally, *all* the stock is not on sale, just the regular stock is on sale. You must speak to the janitor if you want something extra.

The savings are 15 and 20 per cent off. Well, what could be better than that? Except maybe 25. Also on sale, a limited selection of exclusive haberdashery and sportswear, 20 per cent off. You shouldn't go around with 20 per cent of your haberdashery off. But sale or no sale, they won't let you wear it unless it fits. And, boy, do they have fist fights in the front door of that place! The customers are down there screaming, "Let me out! I don't care if it doesn't fit," and they say, "You get back in there!

It's going to fit. Now lie down on that table and shutup! You're not going to get out of here if we have to keep you here all week."

That's the way it is down at Kolmer-Marcus, and if they're listening tonight I don't think Kolmer will be speaking to Marcus in the morning. So remember the address, and I wish I could. Kolmer-Marcus—here it is, Broadway at Thirty-seventh Street, open daily, until night.

All these notes. Let me see here. Here's my notice. Mr. and Mrs. Hy Grund are here.

Frank Martinelli is here. Frank is in a very interesting line. He is a zipper representative. And who among us is not, as a matter of fact?

Hello. Yes, this is Steve Allen. . . . You are an admirer of mine? Well, that's nice. . . . You were worried, you say, about George S. Kaufman? You felt that the industry should have stood behind him to a man? Well, we tried to but it was a little crowded back there.

Station-break time. All right, I don't like to break the station but I may have already. This is WMCA.

Bill Silbert is here. Bill, you like to jump up here for a minute?

SILBERT: I've been watching you work. And I'm tired. You don't feel it? I've also watched you work on two television shows tonight and I want you to know that you are without a doubt.

ALLEN: That's the way I try to work it, Bill, because otherwise the people don't feel that you're giving everything you've got, and who needs it?

SILBERT: Incidentally, there's a very pretty girl that did the commercials on *What's My Line?* tonight. That's the first time, I believe, that *What's My Line?* has had a live commercial.

ALLEN: I've heard a few dead ones on the show.

SILBERT: I won't compete with you. Just go ahead.

ALLEN: To tell you the truth, I'm not competing, either, I'm just functioning in a rather automatic way.

SILBERT: You actually have been sitting here for three hours?

ALLEN: No, for the last hour I've been lying flat on my back.

SILBERT: I think it's amazing, really. You've done two television shows today and you're doing this three hours tonight.

ALLEN: I've got to sneak in a quick commercial or two.

SILBERT: All right. What are we selling, cigarettes?

ALLEN: I don't know. Who is Nat Sherman?

SILBERT: Sells marijuana?

ALLEN: Thanks, Bill. I needed that. Do you know, friends, that you can order Nat Sherman's famous Havana cigarettes by mail? And they won't cost you a penny more. You send them $5.00 and the cigarettes fly to you.

SILBERT: Oh no, he laughs at his own jokes.

ALLEN: What do *I* know? I've got no taste. So, folks, when you smoke, you kill yourself. Why not smoke the finest? That's a good question. I'll be happy to tell you. Sent direct to you from Nat Sherman's huge Spanish cedar-wood humidor.

SILBERT: This is Nat Sherman, not Nat Cole.

ALLEN: Thanks, Bill. I needed that. You and I are going to do a show together sometime, when we're not on the air. When you smoke Sherman's Havana cigarettes, friends, you'll be getting the finest smoke you can get anywhere, so why not keep your mouth shut and keep it to yourself. And don't forget, too, if you want cigarettes or cigars with a special imprint like "It's a Boy," "It's a Girl," or "Get Out of Here" . . . stop in and see Nat Sherman. The address is 1400 Broadway between Thirty-eighth and Thirty-ninth on Chestnut Street. We've got *another* commercial here.

SILBERT: Gosh!

ALLEN: That's it. Friends, have you tried Gosh? The new antisunburn remedy? Rub it on your shoulders and you'll say, "Ooh, Gosh!" Comes in three sizes: small, medium, and *ouch!* It isn't often that an entertainer gets applause from his own sponsor, but Barry has received a letter from his old friend Sam Kamens, even though this commercial was written four years ago. At the Mayflower Hotel in balmy Palm Beach, Florida. Let me read you just this paragraph, "Dear Barry: We were sold out completely for December and for the part that you played in this fine accomplishment my sincere thanks." I'm very sorry I can't get you a room. I know that your audience recognized the unusual value of our December special, which certainly speaks well for their shopping ability. It's a good deal. So if you are interested in having a perfect vacation at a cost well within your nose, phone CIrcle 6-6600 right now for complete details.

SILBERT: What was that number?

ALLEN: I don't know. That's the Mayflower. It's chockful of downright bellboys. I'll get off the air now, because I'm tired. This has been the Barry Gray show featuring Bill Silbert and his orchestra. You were very nice, Bill, all kidding aside, and I'd like to kid you about your side. That's about it for now, ladies and gentlemen. Barry Gray will never be on the air again and we're all parking cars in here in the morning. In the meantime, remember. But I can't remember what. Good night.

THE LATE-SHOW PITCHMAN

One of Allen's TV classics of the early fifties was a takeoff on an advertising spiel that in those days was all over everybody's TV screen—seemingly almost twenty-four hours a day—the now almost forgotten Charles Antell commercial. Its announcers were pitchmen of the old-fashioned sidewalk or dime-store type and Allen was fascinated by their fast-talking, almost hypnotic style. In delivering the following monologue he copied the high-pressure pitchman manner with such success that to this day the TV pitchman is one of his regular TV characters.

Although Allen conceived and wrote much of the Antell takeoff himself, he wishes it known that significant contributions to it were made by Bill Larkin and Larry Markes, writers then on his staff.

* * *

Ladies and Gennemum, make yourselves comfortable and turn up the volume, because I'm going to tell you a big hair-raising story. And when I say BIG I mean BIG, and when I say STORY I mean STORY. Because I am one of the biggest story tellers on the air today!

And correct me if I'm wrong.

For instance, did you know that there are over 500,000 bald women in this country and over ten million bald *men?* The reason you don't notice the bald women is you think they're bald men.

But see my hair? These roots are not dead! Men, are you bald? Does your head keep slipping off the pillow at night?

Do you know what makes you bald? I'll *tell* you what makes you bald. Not having any *hair* makes you bald!

Know what *else* makes you bald? *Worry.* Know what you worry about? Losing your hair!

If you have trouble with your hair, let us get rid of it for you!

When a man starts to lose his hair he usually goes to a baldheaded barber and asks him what he should do. So the barber gets a little perfumed alcohol and sprinkles it on the guy's head. If alcohol could grow hair, most of the men I know would choke to death. *Don't* let the barber pour alcohol on your head! Put it where it'll do the most good. *Drink* it and let it get at the roots of your hair from the *inside.* And let the barber shave your tonsils!

A wonderful exercise is to grab your hair and pull it. Women have better hair than men because the longer hair pulls and strengthens the follicles. Make this interesting test tonight when you get home. Grab your wife's hair and give it a good hard yank. Pull her right off the ground and then let her trickle slowly through your fingers. Now grab *your* hair and pull it. Notice how it burns and irritates as it tears out? Look at your scalp. Is it dry and parched? Now compare your scalp with your neighbor's scalp. For this interesting hobby of collecting and comparing scalps, send for our special Indian knife, with the sharpest edges ever honed.

What do you *ladies* do to your hair? I'll tell you what you do, and correct me if I'm wrong! You dye it, fry it, curl it, swirl it, roast it, toast it, spin it, pin it, oil it, boil it, stuff it, puff it, mash it, smash it, hack it, shellac it, scent it, cement it. You cut it poodle, noodle, apple strudel, every way but Yankee Doodle. You pinch it with pins, and stuff it with cotton, good times there are not forgotten, look away, look away, Dixieland! I wish I was in Dixie! (Pardon me friends, I got carried away.)

As I was saying, ladies, your hair is drenched, wrenched, torched, scorched, incinerated, and embalmed. They take the vitamins and minerals from your hair, they put it in feed for your hogs and cattle. And that's why the pigs that your farmers raise are healthy and win blue ribbons, and the children the farmers raise are rheumatic, diabetic, nervous, and baldheaded!

Scientists have discovered why the women of southern Italy have such wavy hair. You know the reason? Because all through their early years they carry wicker baskets on their heads.

Lots of girls give themselves a home permanent. So they run down to the drugstore and buy themselves a chemistry set. And after they've given themselves a home permanent, they *have* to stay home. Permanent.

This won't happen if you use Charley's Aunt's Formula. Did you know that sheep are the only animals that have to get haircuts? (Next time you're counting sheep notice their hair. You have *never* seen a bald sheep!) The reason is obvious. The sheep use our product. Friends, this formula will grow hair on a billiard ball, if you don't mind playing pool with hairy billiard balls.

Now I'd like to make a little experiment. Here are

three ordinary pieces of writing paper and a bowl of water. I place nothing on the first sheet and dip it into the water. What happens? The paper gets sopping wet. On the second sheet, I place a little mineral oil. And when I dip it in the water, the water runs off, and the mineral oil leaves the paper stained. But, on the *third* piece of paper, I place a little lanolin, and when I dip it in the water the paper rolls up into a tight curl. This proves conclusively that if you want curly writing paper, fill your pen with lanolin!

The same thing happens to sheep on a damp day. There is a natural curl that no amount of pulling or tugging can take out. Ladies, if you want to be seen with curly hair, go out on rainy days with sheep.

Now you saw me put Charley's Aunt on my hair four times during the course of my lecture. I give six or seven lectures a day, six days a week, and I wash my hair two or three times a year. Can you imagine how dirty my hair would be if I didn't have my head drained and the oil changed every thousand miles?

Now watch. Merely by running a damp comb through my hair the waves fall right into place, each one just a little *tighter* than it was before. The same thing happens when it rains. I get tight.

Charley's Aunt's Formula Number 9 contains no harmful ingredients. It does not contain sulphur, or cyanide, or Serutan. It does not contain harsh abrasives, smooth abrasives, latakia, apple honey, irrium, solium, birdseed, nitrates, or day rates. Charley's Aunt contains *lanolin*, the only sheep oil that contains chicken fat! This lanolin is obtained from the backs of happy lambs. They get them happy by feeding them pure grain alcohol, and when the sheep are well oiled, they drain them.

Here's a letter from a satisfied user. She used to be completely bald. Now she has beautiful red hair all the way down her back. Too bad it didn't grow on her head.

Well, you can have a beautiful hair too. And under our sensational offer, you can't lose. You call us at these numbers . . . and a bottle of Charley's Aunt will be sent to you C.O.D. You pay the postman and *he* gives you the shampoo.

And as a special offer, a large, economy-size bottle of our special shampoo, which contains Drano. You put it on and rinse it off four times. It doesn't keep your hair from falling out, but it's awful clean when it hits the floor. Try our amazing thirty-day trial. If you don't bring us to trial in thirty days, we'll be amazed. The price? One can for five bucks, two cans for ten bucks, and our special offer, *five* cans for *ten* bucks.

After using Charley's Aunt's Formula Number 9, ask yourself, "Do I look better?" If your answer is, "WHAAAT, look better?" this offer won't cost you one red cent, because they don't make that color any more.

And now, back to our feature, "The Bowery Boys Meet the Dead End Kids."

ANOTHER WILD NIGHT WITH JIM MORAN

Those who remembered the fabulous Chandler's broadcast that brought together Allen and Jim Moran were overjoyed to discover that several months after the ini-

tial encounter Allen, invited once again to replace Barry
Gray, in turn invited Moran to be his guest.

These two unbelievable interviews—not a word of
which was planned—were the first in a long series of
conversations between Allen and Moran. When Steve
later started the *Tonight* show on NBC he booked the
paunchy publicist as a regular guest and their uninhibited chats provided fans of the *Tonight* program many
an unforgettable moment.

In this instance we are again indebted to Radio Reports, Inc., which recorded the proceedings at Chandler's
restaurant. The transcript opens with the cry of an un-
identified customer who wanted Allen to tell him where
Moran was.

"Where is Jim?" Allen repeated. "Jim who? No, seriously, we all know that Jim is here. Let's hear it for the
great Jim Thorpe, ladies and gentlemen.

"Jim, come up here, will you? Jim is the fabulous publicity and advertising man, the man who has reportedly
sold iceboxes to Eskimos, and found needles in haystacks.

"Jim Moran is now on my right—which makes it very
difficult to jot down notes. There's an obscure remark.
Jim, what new project are you interested in these days?"

MORAN: Nothing now. But did you ever wonder what
sort of a sound a baby kangaroo hears when he is within
his mother's pouch and charging off across the Australian
desert?

ALLEN: Probably something like this. [*He makes a
sound*] Is that close, Jim?

MORAN: No, as a matter of fact, it isn't. That sounds
more like a dugong.

ALLEN: A dugong?

MORAN: A dugong is a perfectly good aquatic mammal.

ALLEN: And it's a good thing that the father dugong eats most of the eggs laid by the mother dugong or you would be up to your ringding in dugongs.

MORAN: Oh, you witty one. But it's not true. As a matter of fact, they don't lay eggs. They're mammals and they give direct birth to their children.

ALLEN: I wouldn't have it any other way. As a matter of fact, I'm a great student of mammalian lore.

MORAN: Well, then you must know about the dugongs. Anyone listening who questions that I have made up a word, look in your dictionary. A dugong is in the whale family, the porpoise family, and they inhabit the waters off of Tasmania, New Guinea, and New Zealand.

ALLEN: You're right, Jim. I was just being facetious.

MORAN: Well, don't do that to me. I'm sensitive. But I wanted to tell you. If you had wondered about these sounds from the pouch of the mother kangaroo, I was in Queensland, Australia, in 1938. I put a little portable broadcasting unit within the pouch of the kangaroo.

ALLEN: What did that kangaroo do?

MORAN: It accepted it. I had it sort of fur-covered. And I stuffed it in this mother's pouch and gave her a slap on what you might call the behind and sent her running off across the veldt.

ALLEN: How many feet of wire did you have?

MORAN: No wire. It's a broadcasting unit, and I sat with a recording unit and a pickup unit and recorded the sounds because I wished—I mean, a human being a little too big to enter this sanctum sanctorum, and wishing to know what these sounds were like, I recorded these sounds, and I have the record at home.

ALLEN: I think this might be the record that could bring back big bands.

MORAN: Bring back what?

ALLEN: Bring back bands. We were talking about bringing back-bands. Do you wear a *back-band*, Jim?

MORAN: No, but I used to *play* in one.

ALLEN: Oh, really? What kind of a band did you play in?

MORAN: I played a bass balalaika in a Greek band. We toured the Near East and played for name days and weddings and various festivals.

ALLEN: Name days?

MORAN: Name days, yes.

ALLEN: Name a day.

MORAN: Well, as you probably know, they don't have birthdays in Greece, the same as with horses . . .

ALLEN: What?

MORAN: Well, you know, horses don't have birthdays. All horses born are considered to be born on January the first of each year.

ALLEN: I think this gives us a cause, Jim.

MORAN: All horses' birthdays are January the first, and all Greeks—instead of their birthdays—have a name day. If your name is Sophocles, all the Sophocleses get together on their name day and they have themselves a ball, and this is where I used to play.

ALLEN: At a Sophocles ball?

MORAN: Yes.

ALLEN: I see. And do Sophocleses come around and say, "You have to buy some tickets to the Sophocles ball or we won't deliver the ice," or whatever they do? What was the instrumentation of your band, besides your bass balalaika?

MORAN: Well, there was a bass (balalaika), about twenty mandolins—

ALLEN: And a dugong.

MORAN: No. Then we had mandolas, what you might call a tenor mandolin, and then we had about, oh, I would say six or seven guitars and a short silver trumpet.

ALLEN: How short?

MORAN: I would say about a nine- or ten-inch trumpet. Really a cornet.

ALLEN: That's more like it, Jim. Who played it?

MORAN: Demetrius played it.

ALLEN: I see. What did Sophocles play?

MORAN: Sophocles was the conductor.

ALLEN: I see, on *"A Streetcar Named Dugong."* What are we talking about? Well, Jim, it's been nice not knowing what's been going on. What are you doing these days? What will you be doing tomorrow at 2:27?

MORAN: Sleeping.

ALLEN: Two thirty-eight?

MORAN: Sleeping.

ALLEN: Anybody make it *three* o'clock? Going. Going. Dugong! What have you got in your pocket, Jim? Pocket Gym, that sounds like a new thing. Little exercisers.

MORAN: You know, my grandfather was one of the pioneers in tape and wire recording. We had this in 1911. I motivated the thing by riding on a bicycle, and we had a piece of metal wire which pulled through two pieces, and my grandfather had the earphones on and was catching the sounds.

ALLEN: What sounds were they?

MORAN: Well, we worked first on plant sounds.

ALLEN: How do they sound?

MORAN: How do plants sound? They sound horrible at times. They're on a different level, as you know, than the human ear, or dogs, or anything like that. For example, you take a mimosa bush trying to grow. You would think this does not make any sound? You would think this is not painful for a mimosa bush to reach maturity?

ALLEN: What does it do—go *ooooh?*

MORAN: Yes, it does, as a matter of fact. And there are mimosa psychologists around who try to ease this pain.

ALLEN: And these are the men we have to watch out for.

MORAN: You sure do. We took a crocus—that's a very easy thing—one time. Well, compared to mimosa. Anybody who's ever been in the sound-recording business knows that.

ALLEN: As a matter of fact, Mimosa Crocus was one of the first artists to record on that label. And a wonderful girl she was.

MORAN: Anyhow, what you have to do is to know where the crocus is coming up, and this takes a sort of a forked stick. I would suggest that you use a forked willow stick. You walk around. Wherever the stick points down, this is where you put the microphone and wait for the crocus to come up.

ALLEN: Well, I'm game if you are. But to get back to the sounds. Have you seen this picture, Jim—what was that Disney thing? *How Green Was My Pool Table,* or what was it? *Nature's Half Acre.*

MORAN: That was the one where they had all of the little insects and animals . . .

ALLEN: Yes, and speeded-up plant growth illustrated graphically.

MORAN: Did they have that? Well, that's the same thing you've got to do with mimosa. You've got to speed it up. In other words, you make a sound recording for, say, half a second, then you wait for about ten minutes, then you take the next one. Otherwise, you're not going to get any continuity in the sound.

ALLEN: I agree with you when you say we've got to speed up the mimosa because I think we've all got to get behind this thing, ladies and gentlemen. If there's anything I can't stand, it's a lazy mimosa.

MORAN: They're growing on their own time. They're like alligators.

ALLEN: Oh? Now you're getting obvious. But what did you mean by that, Jim?

MORAN: Well . . . an alligator has an awfully long time to wait. It's like a turtle.

ALLEN: What is the life span of the alligator?

MORAN: There are people who are going to tell you that a fourteen-foot alligator, for example, is going to live to be five hundred years old. In my own research I have found that an alligator is not good for much more than a hundred and a quarter.

ALLEN: How did you determine this. Unless you stopped daylight-saving time, how did you figure it out?

MORAN: You see, you can write on a turtle's back, and you write 1898 or something. Then you catch this turtle some time four or five hundred years later and this is the way you know. But with an alligator it's a little bit different. An alligator does have a hundred and a quarter to live, and they're quiet people and so they don't get excited about elections or anything.

ALLEN: No. I wonder who the alligators are, Jim—there's a film clip which I've seen in about twenty-seven pictures. In fact, I saw it in *African Queen*, but it was in color and they must have shot the thing fresh. But in all the old Tarzan movies and all pictures like *Abbott and Costello in Africa*, all low-budget African pictures, there's one shot taken about thirty-five feet from the shore. You see about eight alligators sunning themselves, and all of a sudden they go swoosh, down in the water, and all the ushers run out of the theater.

MORAN: Well, all you have to do to get that shot is throw a piece of raw meat in the water. They'll all go down for it.

ALLEN: Let's try that in the kitchen here right now, shall we?

MORAN: You mean have all those lobsters dive for it?

ALLEN: Do you know much about lobsters, Jim?

MORAN: Yes, as a matter of fact, I do. What is the question?

ALLEN: Now that I know, I have none. Hey, I'll tell you something that you might work with me on. Do you dig grunion?

MORAN: As a matter of fact, I do. I have dug grunion. I've *fought* grunion. You know, you *have* to dig them, did you know that?

ALLEN: Yes, or scoop them. And as Walter Winchell can tell you, it's tough to scoop a grunion.

MORAN: To a lot of people listening, this sounds sort of like a joke word, a grunion, but I was kelp inspector on Zuma Beach—

ALLEN: Just a moment, Jim. There are children up. You were a *what* inspector?

MORAN: Kelp inspector on Zuma Beach, for three years in California. That's one of the finest beaches in the world. It's ten miles north of Malibu, and the duties consist of getting up in the morning and walking out to see what's washed up in the way of kelp.

ALLEN: Then you get it out of the way of the kelp so the kelp can get all washed up, is that it? I'm translating for the folks, that's all.

MORAN: So then you see what kelp has come up during the night, and then you walk back and make a report, in a book, and then you go back to sleep. But as you know, during certain times of the moon, the grunions *run* on the Pacific coast, and millions of these small fish about five inches long hit the shore. There is a little publication in Malibu—I think it's called the *Malibu Eagle*—and they tell you when the grunion are going to run, and they'll say that at 12:02 on the night of March 31 the grunion will hit the beach. So you go out and sure enough in come the grunion, but a million of them. They rush in on the beach, and what they're really doing is coming in there and laying eggs. They come up on one wave, and the next wave washes them out, and meanwhile they've laid their eggs real fast. So what you do is catch them while they're in.

ALLEN: That's right. And they never find the eggs.

MORAN: Who never finds the eggs? That's why there're more grunions. The eggs hatch.

ALLEN: And then the new grunions find each other.

MORAN: That's right.

ALLEN: And what do *you* care if you're not a grunion? But one thing I want to ask. We understand about grunion. Now, are you hip to lemmings?

MORAN: Lemmings, yes.

ALLEN: You know what lemmings do? For those who don't, that's a northeastern rodent which goes down to the sea. I happen to be personally of the opinion that in the lemming migrations we find the origin of *The Pied Piper of Hamelin* fable, but that's a digression. The lemmings rush down by the thousands into the North Sea and swim until eventually they drown. There are various theories advanced as to why this occurs. Some people think that it substantiates the claim of a lost continent, that the lemmings have an instinct which indicates to them that they can swim to some other land and then they get there and they find that the land has been taken away and it's very disappointing and so they kill themselves.

Now I have an idea. I propose, Jim—I'm glad we brought up this important subject, too, because there've been matters of very limited interest discussed on this program tonight. I have an idea to import about twenty carloads of lemmings from Norway to the West Coast and line them all up at Malibu and wait till a grunion run is due, and then release the lemmings at the precise moment the grunion are coming up the beach. The lemmings, of course, run out toward the ocean, and can you imagine that crash? Thousands of lemmings and thousands of grunions.

MORAN: You know, some people are going to think we're kidding, but look in your encyclopedias. Look up the lemmings. Look up the grunions, and you'll find that we're not kidding. We haven't made these names up. As a matter of fact, in the Lena River Valley I encountered a large number of lemmings. The Lena River runs out of Siberia into the Arctic Ocean. It has a delta bigger than the Mississippi.

ALLEN: Well, Jim, I think that, when this thing comes up before the union, we'll all be more aware now of how to cast our votes, and I want to thank you very much for enlightening us tonight.

ALLEN WITH ABE BURROWS

Partly because Allen loves to laugh, and partly because he knows comedy inside out, he makes a perfect foil for other comedians. Whether they be established stars or newcomers on the way up they all seem funnier working with Allen than they usually do in other contexts. He enjoys them and the audience reacts to his enjoyment.

The following brief transcript relates the exchange between Steve and Abe Burrows that took place on Allen's CBS radio show on August 13, 1952. At this point he was appearing on both TV and radio and his format in both media was still the casual, unrehearsed, spontaneous, anything-goes structure.

On this occasion he welcomed Burrows (who, though an extremely intelligent man, speaks with the patois of a Brooklyn cabdriver) as "not only a great comic but one of the most inventive minds in the American theater today." In the exchange that follows observe how Allen's amusement at conversational clichés shows through.

* * *

ALLEN: Hiya, Abe!

BURROWS: Hi, Steve.

ALLEN: Abe, where were you born? This is going to be an interview so we might as well face the fact directly.

BURROWS: What do you mean, where was I born? Cambridge, England. Where was I born! What a question! In New York, I was born.

ALLEN: Well, you see, these people are an out-of-town audience. They might not know why you speak the way you do. They're from Wichita, Cincinnati, Peoria . . .

BURROWS: I know there are a lot of people from out of town. I know there are some *places* out of town. I understand there's a *lot* of out of town. I've never really *been* out of town. If I go to Newark I get nervous. I understand there's a whole country, a lot of states and cities out of town.

ALLEN: Yes, they're really opening it up.

BURROWS: And it's the turnpikes that are doing it.

ALLEN: I was reading an angry letter the other night (speaking of turnpikes) and somebody had a wonderful idea. They said when it's crowded on Sunday afternoons why don't they open *all* the lanes instead of having one miserable cop with three hands accepting the dimes.

BURROWS: There's a good reason why they don't do that.

ALLEN: Why?

BURROWS: It makes sense. That upsets them very much. You see, if there were no traffic jams what would they do? The *idea* of a turnpike is to have a whole new road which will create a clean, outdoor traffic jam.

ALLEN: And get it out of the city.

BURROWS: Certainly. You don't want a traffic jam right in town. In Newark they built something called the Pulaski Skyway. That's so you can have a traffic jam *high up*.

ALLEN: Where were you born, Abe?

BURROWS: In the city of Manhattan, which was later incorporated into New York. I was born downtown. There's a whole thing too—downtown. Later we moved *up*town and then I moved to Brooklyn and that is where I finally learned to talk decently.

ALLEN: What were your early ambitions?

BURROWS: To talk decently. No, my mother wanted me to be a doctor. So today I cut my thumb.

ALLEN: How?

BURROWS: With a knife. What do you mean, how? I cut myself with a microphone?

ALLEN: You could have stuck it in a pencil sharpener for all I know.

BURROWS: Well, anyway, I lived in Brooklyn and had early ambitions, like you said, and I grew up and then something happened and I went into show business.

ALLEN: How did you get into show business? I understand you first used to sell labels.

BURROWS: I did.

ALLEN: What kind of labels? Beer-bottle labels?

BURROWS: *Clothing* labels. Like this, it says in the coat, see? I sold woven labels.

ALLEN: Who wove them?

BURROWS: A firm. You've got a label in your suit. See what it says? "Property of Salvation Army." I went into show business for the same reason I sold labels—to make a living.

ALLEN: I understand the original step was taken as a result of your being pushed by entertainers who were convulsed by your antics at parties. Abe would sit down at a piano with a lot of comedians in the room and he'd be the funniest one there and it was embarrassing to the comedians to be topped by an amateur so they got him into show business.

BURROWS: Well, first I was a writer. Then I became an actor and after acting a few years I'm back to writing again. You know, I've been writing and directing Broadway shows. Now I'm doing a new show with Cole Porter.

ALLEN: What's the name of it?

BURROWS: *Can-can.*

ALLEN: Who plays the part of the hyphen? Abe is the man who wrote *Guys and Dolls*. He's also written lots of wonderful songs. What are the names of your big songs?

BURROWS: You mean "The Girl with the Three Blue Eyes"? Then there are titles like "I Was Walking Down the Memory Lane Without a Single Thing to Remember." And, oh, I wrote one the other week, a thing that starts off "Yesterday they told you you would not go far. Last night you opened, and they were right." I got one called "How Are You Going to Keep Them Down on the Farm after They've Seen the Farm?"

This is quite pleasant. Come on, interview me some more.

ALLEN: All right. Where were you born? But actually, Abe. That about does it. That's about the size of it. That's the way she goes, as a matter of fact.

BURROWS: You're just stuck. I can tell because when my father was stuck he always said, "Well, that's the way she goes."

ALLEN: I had an uncle who had a great line at such moments. He'd stand up and stretch and he'd sigh, "Oh, lordy, lordy, lordy, lordy." Everybody's uncle has a line like that.

BURROWS: When it gets quiet in a room somebody says, "Well, whaddaya gonna do?"

ALLEN: A question we hear all too often these days.

BURROWS: Well, whaddaya gonna do?

ALLEN: Oh, lordy, lordy, lordy, lordy!

BURROWS: So, what's going to be?

ALLEN: Abe, you can say that again.

BURROWS: I don't *want* to say it again.

ALLEN: Anybody tuning in late, we sound like Walter O'Keefe doing his old act.

BURROWS: Uh-uh.

ALLEN: Uh-uh? First time I've ever been topped by a growl.

BURROWS: Say, you know the Giants are losing.

ALLEN: What giants?

BURROWS: The Giants are never troubled for new comedy material. They just lose. They're losing to the

Cubs. And the Dodgers are getting murdered by, of all people—

ALLEN: The Harlem Globe Trotters.

BURROWS: No, the Pittsburgh Pirates. You know what it *means* to get beat by the Pittsburgh Pirates? It's like if Milton Berle gets quieted down by Jack Lescoulie. No, really, the Pirates are beating them. I was quite depressed.

ALLEN: Do you bet on the games?

BURROWS: Betting is not permitted.

ALLEN: So why are you depressed?

BURROWS: Because betting is not permitted. Well, whaddaya gonna do?

ALLEN: You know, I have a confession to make. When I was a little boy in Chicago I could tell you who played every position on every team and what his batting average was. You know why? Because I used to chew cheap gum and save baseball cards.

Really, I still have a collection of Max Bishop and Paul Waner cards. I even remember Guy Bush.

BURROWS: So what's the matter? You don't chew gum no more?

ALLEN: Well, it's the teeth, Abe. They're going. No. Somebody stole my card collection and it depressed me and I haven't been interested in baseball since.

BURROWS: Gee, that's tough. Well, that's the way she goes.

ALLEN: Well, Abe . . . hey, I just did something people do on the phone. Did you ever notice when a fellow calls you—you may talk for about twenty minutes but you can always tell when he's through because he says the word "well."

BURROWS: That's after twenty minutes. With me I say, "Hello, George, this is Abe. Well?" Really, trying to get off a phone is a problem with a lot of people.

ALLEN: I don't even *like* the telephone because of that. I hate the pauses.

BURROWS: You've practically got to say to a guy, "Well, look, I've got a fire in the living room." I'm a guy who has a great deal of difficulty telling the truth in social intercourse. I can't say to a guy, "Look, I don't want to talk to you any more." None of us has that much nerve. So what you do? You say, "Well, my mother is sick"— or—"My hat's on fire." You always lie. It's a terrible habit to get into.

ALLEN: I don't know. It saves people a little pain.

BURROWS: Well look, Steve, there's a fire at my house.

ALLEN: And your mother's sick and your uncle's hat is smoking.

BURROWS: But it doesn't save them pain, really. If you said to a guy, "Look, I think we've talked enough, don't you? Good-bye. Thanks," that's much kinder, because if you say, "Well, I've got to run along now. I have to go and fix the turnpike," then the guy hangs up and he says, "I'll bet that guy didn't want to talk to me."

He says, "What was he giving me—the brush?" He'll build up a burn. Honesty is always the best policy.

ALLEN: It's better to make a clean break, is that your idea? I used to know a woman on the West Coast. As a matter of fact, I worked for her awhile. Her name is Chloe Owing. She was the head of a radio school there. Chloe had a rather interesting telephone habit. She never said good-bye. When she was through she would just hang up. Period. It was fine for her but it made for about twenty minutes of trouble for the operator. You were always sure you had been disconnected and when you'd call back Chloe'd say, "Oh, what do you want now?"

BURROWS: Really, we should campaign for honesty. I used to have a friend, a producer in Hollywood, who could never say no. A guy would say, "Hey, Jack, come to my house for dinner Thursday?" He'd lie and say, "I can't Thursday. I'm going to San Francisco." And then a week would go by—you know what he would do? It's a true story. He'd go to San Francisco. This guy was always trapped by his own stories.

ALLEN: And, friends, that man today is mayor of San Francisco. So it just goes to show that *dis*honesty is the best policy.

Abe, it was swell of you to come in tonight and give us of your time and talent.

4

THE *TONIGHT* SHOW IS BORN

After Allen came to a parting of the ways with CBS in 1953, he was active in a variety of other areas (including an acting appearance on the Broadway stage in *The Pink Elephant*). But in 1954 a move was made that was to prove decisive in establishing him once and for all as one of the most popular and gifted men in national television.

After several months of negotiations, the Ruppert Knickerbocker Beer Company agreed to sponsor Allen in an informal nightly show to be seen locally on the NBC New York outlet. The station provided Allen with Bobby Byrne and his orchestra (eventually to be replaced by Skitch Henderson) and announcer Gene Rayburn. Several singers were auditioned, including a seventeen-year-old lad named Steve Lawrence, who was with the show from the start. A few weeks later a girl singer named Eydie Gorme was added. The following year Andy Williams became a member of the family.

"The program seemed to fill a need," says Steve, "among people who were tired of a nightly diet of old Charlie Chan movies. For the first time since coming to New York I felt completely in my element in television because the new program was conducted very much along the lines of my old Hollywood radio show. There was little script, though two great writers, Stan Burns and Herb Sargent, contributed some fine sketches and jokes. But the show was mostly ad-lib chatter, audience interviews, piano music, and songs from Steve, Eydie, and the band. Within a few months Pat Weaver, NBC's chief at the time, called me in and said that he planned to put the program on the network."

The *Tonight* show achieved a rare balance in that it was capable, under Allen's subtly skilled guidance, of appealing to viewers of every intellectual level.

Since Allen talked almost incessantly for the next three years, five nights a week, ninety minutes a night, it would be essentially a hopeless task to attempt to present here not only the best of his material—it would fill volumes— but even a small representative sampling that would give the full flavor of the original *Tonight* show. Years later when Jack Paar took it over he initiated the policy of surrounding himself with four or five guests, which made it almost possible for Paar to phone in his part of the as- signment. Allen, on the other hand, worked mostly alone, or with his studio audience, or with eccentric guests. About the best one can do in this sort of anthology is present a few typical Allen cracks of the period and just say: this is how it was every night.

A physician in the audience asked Allen one evening if he was allergic to anything. "Yes," Allen said, truthfully. "I'm allergic to two things, cigars and dogs. And if I ever meet a dog smoking a cigar I'll be in *real* trouble."

Another night a group of Pittsburghers were extolling their city's virtues and seemed particularly anxious to correct the popular misconception of Pittsburgh as a dirty town.

"Years ago," one man told Steve, "Pittsburgh used to be the dirtiest city in the United States, but it's not any more. And do you know why?"

"Yes," said Allen, "it's because St. Louis has gotten much dirtier."

When a guest observed that a certain attractive actress had "a very healthy constitution," Steve said, "Yes, and the amendments to it are rather impressive, too."

During a discussion of diets, a lady guest said with great zeal, "I don't believe in vitamin pills."

"But," said Steve, with mock sincerity, "I've *seen* them."

Part of an interview between prize fighter Floyd Patterson and Steve:

STEVE: What is your daughter's name?

FLOYD: Seneca.

STEVE: How did you happen to select such an unusual name?

FLOYD: Well, my wife and I were trying to decide on a name for the baby and one day we happened to be walking down this street in Brooklyn and we looked up at the street sign and it said Seneca. So, that was it.

STEVE: You're lucky you weren't walking on Flatbush Avenue.

A young man in his studio audience said to Steve one evening, "As a TV star do you resent it when characters try to get on your show just to bask in your reflected glory?"

"Well," Allen conceded, "I do resent some of those baskers."

His producer Bill Harbach once asked, "Whatever happened to Frank Buck? Is he still working?"

"No," Steve said, "he was badly clawed last year by Clyde Beatty."

One evening Sugar Ray Robinson was to be interviewed from his training camp in upstate New York. During the afternoon, while they were rehearsing, microphone trouble developed and the director asked Steve to keep talking into his mike while they adjusted the volume. Steve resorted to the radio custom of counting into the microphone to save wear and tear on his mind while the engineers fixed the mike.

"One, two, three, four, five, six, seven, eight, nine, ten," he said, looking at Robinson on the TV screen. Then, without pausing for breath, he added, "Nothing personal, Sugar."

Once, doing the show in Miami Beach, Allen heard a clothier say to another, as a young woman strolled past wearing overly tight slacks, "I realize now I should have added Capri pants to our line."

"Hindsight," was Steve's comment.

If there is any one incident that fully captures the flavor of the old *Tonight* show it is this: Allen was demonstrating the virtues of a nonbreakable Fiberglas chair. The manufacturer had told him he could take a hammer and strike the chair as hard as he wished to demonstrate its indestructibility. With the first whack, Allen poked a hole right through the chair. Hysteria didn't reign in the audience—it poured.

Steve got himself out of the hole with what I consider a classic ad lib. "Well, anyway," he explained, "this *hammer* is made of Fiberglas."

* * *

THE *TONIGHT* SHOW

At the end of our first season the *Tonight* program was, as I had expected, put on the full NBC network, after which it ran for two more years. The three seasons that our gang held down the time spot were wonderfully happy. A separate book could be written about the program, but for now I'll have to content myself with just reminiscing about its highspots and about some of the people who came into my life as a result of the show. Dwight Hemion, my TV director, was part of the team almost from the first, as was Bill Harbach, our producer. These two young men have never gotten the credit they deserve for the success of both the late-night show and the once-a-week program that followed it. Bill is a cheerful enthusiast with a wonderful, albeit whacky, manner of handling people and getting their best work out of them. Best of all, considering that he is producing comedy shows, he loves to laugh.

But without knowing it, Bill is funny himself. He does not mean to be. He is not a jokester or a cutup. But something about his ferretlike nervous system and a certain difficulty in expressing himself when he is excited combine to make him say some of the most outlandish things this side of Sam Goldwyn.

One day while involved in a heated debate with Jules Green, our executive producer, Bill hit the ceiling at one of Jules' suggestions. "There you go, Jules," he shouted. "For the first time you're wrong again!"

Another time, wanting to conclude our program with a

religious number that was not too slow in tempo, he came running in to my office and said, "What's a good *up* hymn?"

And, under the same general heading, there was the day he attempted to enumerate the Holy Trinity. "You know," he explained, "the Holy Father, Your Son, and the Ghost."

I should perhaps remind the reader that he says things of this sort with a perfectly straight face, and in all seriousness.

Once, in Havana, Cuba, when Jules inquired as to what time the various members of our group were dispersing to return home, Bill replied, "I'm dispersing Wednesday."

Then there was the day he came into my office to discuss something about the program and I noticed he was wearing a heavy overcoat. "Do you have a chill?" I said.

"No," he said. "Why?"

"Well," I said, "you're walking around indoors with your coat on."

"Oh," he said, in surprise, "I forgot to take it off. No! I forgot to go home." And with that he dashed out of the room and ran for the elevator.

Another peculiarity of Bill's is that he has the world's worst memory for names. Not only does he forget them, but, tantalizingly enough, some shred of their memory remains in his mind, causing him to cry out strange variations upon names he is trying to call to mind. Instructing his secretary to call Charlton Heston for rehearsal one afternoon, he shouted, "Get me—uh—Charleston Huston. Er, uh—Carleton Hudson. You know, Chester Moses."

And another time, when we were talking about doing a show from a swimming pool, he said, "There's only one guest to book for a show like that . . . whatsername . . . Ethel Waters." Naturally he meant Esther Williams.

He has also been known to refer to the comedy ice-skating team of Fric and Frac as Trick or Treat and he has called Shai K. Ophir, the brilliant mime, Ootie Shankar. Even stranger to relate, he has been heard to say, "When is Christmas?" while standing looking at the month of December on a calendar, and to ask, "How many feet in a foot?" while estimating the dimensions of a set.

But the strangest thing I ever heard him say was a brief phrase he mumbled one afternoon as he excused himself from a production meeting: "Let me be right back."

Jules Green was my agent for a good many years, since the old Hollywood days, and, like Bill, he is something of a character and frequently amusing without intending to be. Like Bill, too, he sometimes lets his emotion run away with his tongue. For example, in talking about an unpopular political figure who died and for whom someone in the room was expressing mild sympathy, Jules snapped, "To hell with him. There are dead men walking the streets tonight because of him!"

Two writers who have been with me since the old local New York days are Stan Burns and Herb Sargent. They, too, seem like a couple of characters out of fiction. Stan is a big, husky ex-Marine with the pleasantest personality in the world. In twelve years I have never known him to have a glum moment, and his wife and children seem as jovial as he. Oddly enough his speciality in comedy is what has come to be known as the Sick Joke. His subject matter is apt to include death, Hitler, accidents, national catastrophes, and the like. Needless to say, some of his most impressive jokes could never be used on the air. He was the originator, for example, of that much-quoted Sick classic, "Remember folks, ——————— Airlines is the Airline of the Stars. Carole Lombard, Grace Moore, Will Rogers . . ." And I was not surprised one afternoon while on a plane with Stan to see him wandering up and down the aisle with a small box of sweets borrowed from a stewardess.

"After-crash mints, anyone?" he was saying.

His partner, Sargent, also a brilliant joke-smith (recently producer of *That Was the Week That Was*) is tall, dark, and quiet. Given to wearing tweed sports jackets, he has the short Connecticut haircut, the grizzled Ivy League look of the men in the cigarette ads. While lost in thought he may stand in the middle of the room shrugging his shoulders and quietly flapping his fingers, arms held slightly out from his sides. When I go into his office to talk to him I often do this gesture. He laughs and then we go on with the conversation. I say *go on* rather than *start,* for in our office conversations are never really begun or concluded. They all seem to begin in the middle, taking off from some point of earlier reference, and are invariably broken off in mid-sentence or interrupted by another party. This has been the case, oddly enough, from the very first days of the late-night TV show.

The show itself, seen in retrospect, brings up a great many memories. For example, there were the *regulars* of the studio audience, those hardy souls who seemed to have no purpose in life but to spend every waking moment—and some sleeping ones—at one or another radio or TV show. Most M.C.'s avoid them like the plague and issue stern instructions that they are to be cattle-penned off to the rear seats. Personally I like the regulars. They entertain and amuse me. They do the same, I think, for audiences watching at home. Given a choice between a regular and an unknown quantity represented, let's say, by a stranger in a gray suit sitting on the aisle, I'll head for the regular eight times out of ten. It isn't just that I get more mileage out of the steady customers; it's that I'm constantly on the lookout for the person who seems eccentric, extroverted, and willing to talk, and that's a good description of a regular.

One of our most dependable steadies on the *Tonight* show was an elderly lady of obviously small financial means known simply as Mrs. Sterling. I do not know her first name to this day. I do not know where she lives. I think perhaps she still lives in the fourth row of NBC's Hudson Theatre and goes home only about once a month to change clothes.

Like most of the regulars, she was present nightly partly because she liked the show and partly (and perhaps predominantly) because she liked to carry home loot and knew that I gave things away to the people I interviewed.

Mrs. Sterling had a simple act, but it seemed invariably to amuse audiences. First she complimented me lavishly, then she demanded a gift, usually a "Pomeroy" camera. The camera's name is actually Polaroid, but Mrs. Sterling wasn't particular. Our conversations, which rarely varied, went something like this:

I: Good evening, Mrs. Sterling. How are you this evening?

MRS. S: Mr. Allen, you're wonderful.

I: That may well be, Mrs. Sterling, but I didn't come

over here to listen to your compliments again, flattering as they are.

MRS. S: But I just want everybody to know what an angel you are, Mr. Allen. I hope you're feeling well.

I: But Mrs. Sterling, I—

MRS. S: You're not working too hard, are you?

I: Up until this moment I wasn't, no.

MRS. S: That's fine. Say, I'd like to have one of those Pomeroy cameras.

I don't recall just now whether I ever actually gave Mrs. Sterling a camera, but we did lavish upon her a rich assortment of stockings, record albums, salamis, wrist watches, perfumes, furniture, and electric appliances. I don't know whether she used these articles, sold them, or stored them away on the Collier brothers plan.

Not content, by the way, with demanding things for herself, Mrs. Sterling usually demanded seconds for "my daughter." Several people on our staff suspected there was no daughter, but we nevertheless from time to time gave Mrs. Sterling two of this and that so that her daughter, if any, might not be disappointed.

Our at-home viewers became so intrigued by Mrs. Sterling's insistence that I supply gifts for her daughter that once when a fan sent us a gold cup inscribed "To Mrs. Sterling" it was followed two days later by a small cup from another watcher. The second one was engraved "For Mrs. Sterling's Daughter."

One thing that our millions of viewers never knew is that from time to time Mrs. Sterling used to lurk outside the theater waiting for me to appear. When I did she would rush up and hand me a small paper bag or package.

It would contain a present, usually handkerchiefs or candy, from her to me.

Another regular who visited us two or three nights a week for almost a year was a tall, thin man named John Schafer. To say that John talked a lot doesn't remotely give you the idea. Schafer had a long-playing tongue. I stumbled over him one night in the audience and started a conversation with the usual "And what's your name, sir?"

"Well," he said, speaking extremely rapidly, "my name is Schafer. John Schafer. I work as a farmer upstate. That is, it's not *my* farm, you understand, but my uncle's farm, but I figure eventually it'll be my farm. I mean if everything turns out all right. We raise quite a few nice things on the farm. It's about a hundred acres and we've been up in that section for the last two, three generations. I just come down to town once in a while to see the sights and have a little fun. Watch your show once in a while and thought I'd drop in and see it. What was it you wanted to ask me?"

"To tell you the truth, Mr. Schafer," I said, "I had five or six questions in mind but you've already answered all of them."

John came in quite regularly and one night I happened to ask him where he'd been the night before.

"Well," he said, "I seen this movie, *Mogambo,* with Clark Gable and this Ava Gardner woman and it was a pretty good picture, but to tell you the truth I couldn't figure out what old Clark was so interested in this Gardner woman for when I figgered he would've been better off with this blond girl, whatsername, this Kelly girl. Her father's from Philadelphia. 'Course it sure was something when all those old gorillas came running around and old Clark had to step lively to keep things on an even keel."

John went on lickety-split in that vein for about five minutes, during which time I did not say a single word. When he finished I said, "So that's what you did last night, eh?"

But I realized there was more value to John's monologues than met the eye. Not only were they the longest straight lines in the history of comedy, but his synopses of motion pictures had a childlike charm. We signed him up for a series of movie reviews, which were well received by our audiences, if not by the motion picture companies.

Perhaps our most unusual regular was a gentleman we discovered one summer when we originated the program in Hollywood. The customary query as to his identity he brushed aside with the immediate suggestion that he sing a song for us. He was a short, stocky man with a heavy and, to me, still unidentifiable accent. His name, I later learned, was Carmen Mastren.

"What song would you like to sing?" I asked.

"'Allagazanada's Ragatima Band,'" he said.

"What key do you sing in?" I asked, hoping to pick up a cue for Skitch Henderson, who was at that time our conductor.

"A," Carmen said. He sang every song in the key of A, it developed, or at least he *said* he did. Actually we never could figure out what key he sang in because he did every song *on one note*.

Another fascinating visitor to our studios was a little old man named Ben Belefonte. He called himself a rhyming inventor. This does not mean that he invented

...and the champion's rabbit punches are finally beginning to tell on Petroni.

The ball is now in Oklahoma territory.

rhymes, but rather that he was an inventor who incidentally happened to write rhymes. I shall never forget his
weird inventions. One of them was a hanger bank. This
was not a device for hanging banks and it did not bank
hangers. It was simply a common-variety, transparent
plastic hanger in which Mr. Belefonte had cut some holes
large enough to permit the passage of small coins. You
simply dropped pennies, nickels, and dimes into the
hanger until it was full and then you had a hanger full of
coins. Don't ask me who would need such a device.

Ben spoke in rhymed but not rhythmic verse and undoubtedly his most fantastic invention was a rhyme that
had never fallen from the lips of man before and I'm sure
never will again. He somehow managed to make the
word *the* rhyme with the word *inventor* by saying:

> "I'm Ben Belefonte, *the*
> Rhyming inven*tuh!*"

Another wild character was a man known as Professor
Voss, who years later was to pop up again on my Westinghouse show. The professor was a well-preserved man
in his late sixties. He spoke with a slight Germanic accent, liked to walk around with a bare chest in the coldest
weather, and had some very unusual ideas about diet
and exercise. One night a dreadful thing he said made
the audience laugh for such a long time that I am sorry
somebody didn't time the laugh with a stopwatch.

"Tell me, professor," I said, as he sat in a large tub
filled with ice floating in freezing cold water, "to what
do you attribute your remarkable physical condition?"

"Well," he explained. "It's water that does it. You've got
to start off each day by drinking plenty of water."

"Do you do that?" I said.

"Oh yes, indeed," he said. "The first thing you must do when you get up in the morning is drink four quarts of water!"

"Wow," I said. "Four quarts. That's a lot of water. And what do you do then?"

"Well," he said, as matter-of-factly as if he were discussing the weather, "you stand about three feet from the toilet—"

Naturally I cut him off immediately, but there was no stopping the audience.

Another night that there was no stopping them one of our staff had booked as a guest a woman who was an expert on the care and feeding of cats. She had brought about twelve cats to the studio and on my desk she had placed a sort of doll's house, in and around which five or six of the cats were crawling, playing, sleeping, and what-have-you. As soon as I walked into the theater and saw this setup the word "cathouse" flashed across my mind so I gathered Skitch Henderson, Gene Rayburn, Steve Lawrence, Eydie Gorme, and the rest of our crew around me.

"Be sure," I instructed, "that when we start talking to this lady about her cats and the little house that they are playing in . . . be sure that *no one* uses the word cathouse." They chuckled at the possibility and all, of course, at once agreed that the dread word would not fall from their lips.

A few minutes later we went on the air and shortly thereafter I began to interview the woman who had brought all the cats.

"What is this thing?" I said, pointing to the little house.

"Oh, that," she said amiably. "That's a cathouse."

Another *Tonight* regular that people still ask me about was Joe Interleggi, whom I dubbed The Human Termite because he ate wood. Well, he didn't actually digest it, I suppose, but Joe's claim to fame was that he had jaws and teeth of such prodigious strength that he could bite holes in any piece of wood in the house. And he could. He could also open beer bottles with his teeth and then grind the bottle caps into small, twisted wads by rolling them around in his mouth. A native of Italy, Joe became tremendously popular with our viewers.

And there are so many other familiar faces that I recall with pleasure. There was Mrs. Dorothy Miller, a plump and pleasant lady in her fifties who has been sitting in my audiences now for about sixteen years, having started in Hollywood. And there is a woman known only as "Lillian," who also has seen many years of faithful service in the audience. The fantastic thing about Lillian was that *wherever* we went, she showed up. When we did the *Tonight* show once at Niagara Falls there she was, smiling up from the front row. And she followed our circus to Havana, to Hollywood, to Texas. We never knew how she got her tickets, how she managed to get a front-row seat, or where she stayed in the various cities to which she followed us. But there she was. When I moved my program and staff to Hollywood in 1959 she made that trip with us, too, staying in town for several weeks, although she eventually had to return to her home in New York.

And what wild nights there were on the old *Tonight* show, what crazy ad-lib routines. One of my favorites, because it was true, extemporaneous, and unpredictable comedy, was that in which we used to open the back door of the theater and just point a TV camera out into the night. Passers-by, having no idea that they could be seen on television from coast to coast, would saunter by, do a double take, and then casually, oh so casually, drift back and look into the theater, which meant, of course, that they were looking right into the camera.

After a few minutes drunks would pile out of the neighborhood saloons and wave at the camera deliberately, and then it would be time to end the routine, but those first few minutes were always priceless. I would keep a microphone open and make off-the-cuff comments on the various faces that loomed up on the screen, like strange fish floating before a submerged camera. If you never saw this routine it will be difficult to explain just why it was funny. But take my word for it, it was.

Another routine of the old *Tonight* show that used to be a great favorite was that in which we would suddenly open the back door, point a camera outside, and then I would walk quickly out into the night dressed in some peculiar costume and try to engage passers-by in conversation. The wildest thing that ever happened on the show under this particular heading, I guess, occurred the night that I dressed in a policeman's uniform, ran out on the street, and began stopping automobiles. I had no idea what I was going to say to the drivers, but I figured that just the sheer, insane idea of stopping actual cars on live TV and saying *anything* would make for unusual fare.

Since I had lived in the west and had on several occasions been stopped by the state police guard on the Arizona-California border, it was perhaps not surprising that I now heard myself saying to the first driver who slowed down, "Sorry, sir, but this is the border patrol and we're making a spot check for contraband."

"What band?" he said. Since the bright lights from the theater prevented his seeing the TV cameras, or for that matter from even recognizing that the building to his left was a theater, he had no reason to doubt that I was an actual policeman.

"I just wanted to know," I said, "if you're smuggling any fruits or nuts."

"No," he said. "Absolutely not." From inside the theater came a great roar of laughter.

"Drive on," I said, "and remember, the life you save . . . may not be worth it."

When I raised my hand to stop the next car its driver suddenly stepped on the gas and sped by me, almost knocking me down. This, too, the audience found vastly amusing.

"Border patrol," I shouted to the driver of the third car. "Are you smuggling anything?"

"No, sir," he said, blinking at the lights.

"Well, then," I cried, signaling to an associate who brought me an oversized salami, "take this to the river!"

"To the what?" he said, accepting the salami.

"Never mind," I shouted. "Just get going. And don't stop till you hear from me!" He sped off as if possessed.

The next car to come along was a taxi. I grabbed another salami and flagged the driver down. "Where to, chief?" he said, amiably.

"Never mind," I said, opening his back door and flinging the salami in. "Just take this to Grand Central, and fast!" Oddly enough he sped off at once into the night. The audience laughed so loudly that it sounded like a cheer from a football stadium. We never heard from the driver after the show and I have often wondered why he shot off down Forty-fifth Street that way, following such an insane order.

* * *

END OF AN ERA

By 1955 NBC had Allen doing not only the *Tonight* program but also a full comedy hour Sunday nights at eight o'clock opposite Ed Sullivan. About this same time, he somehow also managed to star in the *Benny Goodman Story* for Universal-International. But the pace proved killing, even for the energetic Allen. Reluctantly he decided to give up the *Tonight* program. At first the network asked him to do at least three nights a week, giving up just two. He suggested either Jack Paar or Ernie Kovacs as his replacement and the NBC brass chose Kovacs. But after a few months Allen had to quit *Tonight* entirely. Rather than continue without him NBC canceled the program. The outpouring of grief at the passing of the show was nationwide, and genuine. Joe Reilly, columnist for the Brockton *Daily Enterprise,* of Brockton, Massachusetts, expressed the general sentiment well:

"'Heigho-Stevo, and good night, Sweet Prince.' That telegram from Louis Nye just about wrapped it up on the occasion of Steve Allen's departure from TV's *Tonight.* It summed up succinctly our emotions as we sat watching Allen ring down his final curtain with the good taste and restraint that are hallmarks of his personality and humor. Sure, now and again tears filled our eyes. The good-byes packed an emotional wallop. But we were cheered that the young man was moving onward and upward.

"Allen's good-byes to his country-wide *Tonight* fans were touching—because they were from the heart, without the least sign of self-dramatization. No touch of the maudlin was in evidence, although it would have been so easy to have been swung in that direction. Steve recognized, for instance, the deprivation his departure meant to shut-ins and the like. He said so. You could tell it truly grieved him that that's the way the cards fell. In all likelihood he valued those fans beyond all others. That seems to be the nature of the man. But he bade them good-bye, man-fashion, with a cushion of affection. Tempering the blow was the fact he'll still be around on Sunday nights.

"By this time you're aware that I hold Steve Allen in considerable esteem. If you don't happen to go for him, that's okay, too. It takes all kinds to make a world, they say. But his particular brand of comedy I like, and I admire a man who can dish it out—the trite and the tripe he steers away from in favor of the novel and many times even the bizarre. He knew what he liked to see and hear over television.

"He grasped the opportunity to boost talented newcomers. Even some not so talented. He was bound that they would have a hearing. They did. It was interesting to watch their development under Steve's banner. Eydie Gorme and young Steve Lawrence, for example. They came a long way. So did others. They all have Allen to thank.

"For some time the word was around that the Allen format of *Tonight* was doomed. If he was out, so was the program. There was no one to replace him. It just wasn't the same show without Allen."

Critic John Crosby also lamented the fact that Allen had given up the *Tonight* show.

"There will be a *Tonight* show next year, but it won't be the show as we know it. Or to be more specific, Steve Allen won't be on it, and I'll miss that special quality he brought to it.

"The Allen humor is an offhand, throwaway, irrelevant type of humor that is hard to imitate and even harder to explain. Once when he was explaining that the West Coast saw his show by kinescope, he said, 'The program is seen out there three hours later—due to carelessness.' I don't know why that amuses me, except that it seems to poke a hole in all our electronic wonders of today—kinescope, television, the whole works.

"There is no situation I've ever seen that Allen couldn't rise above—and there have been some pretty wild ones. Once, for example, a well-upholstered young lady who was demonstrating a mattress explained she was 'Miss Foam Bedding of 1957.'

"That title, I think, would have struck me speechless. I simply wouldn't know how to continue a conversation with a girl who announced she was Miss Foam Bedding of 1957. But Allen had the perfect gambit.

" 'What happened to Miss Foam Bedding of 1956?' " he asked.

" 'She's not with us any more,' " said Miss Foam Bedding of 1957.

"As I say, I'll miss it.

"Louis Nye, one of Allen's greatest discoveries, was on hand for the final broadcast. 'Steve,' he said, 'this marks the end of an era in television.'

"He was right."

BACK TO LATE-NIGHT

The *Tonight* show was 5 per cent script and 95 per cent ad lib. The *Steve Allen Show,* a Sunday evening series that ran for four seasons (1956–1960), reversed these propositions; in fact, it had a staff of seven writers.

Allen worked closely as editor of the scripts, and made contributions of his own, but he has always insisted on giving full credit to the various joke-smiths who created the bulk of the written material for the program. Most students of TV comedy consider that the two most creative, original, and influential comedy programs of the past fifteen years were the *Sid Caesar Show* and the *Steve Allen Show.* Interestingly enough, Caesar is Allen's own favorite comedian. Steve considers Sid "the Chaplin of television."

The Allen show won a Peabody Award in 1960 as best comedy show of the year, a fact for which Steve gives much credit not only to his writers—Stan Burns, Herb Sargent, Leonard Stern, Don Hinkley, Bill "Jose Jimenez" Dana, Arnie Sultan, and Marv Worth—but also to the great cast of supporting comics who worked with him during his years with NBC (and his one season on ABC): Dana, Louis Nye, Don Knotts, Tom Poston, Gabe Dell, Pat Harrington, Jr., Dayton "Why Not?" Allen, and Tim Conway. Other comedians who have worked with Allen on TV—many of whom received either their first or most important exposure with him—were Shelley Berman, Jim Nabors, Don Adams, Mort Sahl, Mike Nichols and Elaine May, Jonathan Winters, Lenny Bruce, the Smothers Brothers, Jackie Mason, Jackie Vernon, Grecco and Willard, Jack Sheldon, Fred Smoot, and Bill Daley.

Since this book is concerned not with the humor simply *performed* by Steve Allen but rather with the humor created or written by him, it is appropriate at this point to segue directly to the Steve Allen Westinghouse show, a series that brought Allen back, in June 1962, to the five-nights-a-week television world and to the informality that had characterized *Tonight*.

The Westinghouse program, which ran for almost two and a half years on various stations from coast to coast as well as in Australia and Canada, differed from *Tonight* in a few respects. The most striking change was the greatly increased reliance on visual, physical comedy. More than ever before Allen manipulated himself into strange situations, many of them of an athletic and sometimes quite dangerous nature. Performed either onstage or in the streets surrounding his studio on Hollywood's Vine Street, these stunts were aimed more at the direct belly laugh than at subtle and cerebral appeal. One night Steve might try to become a tightrope walker high above La Mirada Avenue and Vine; another night he might play piano while swinging in midair from a crane, or scale a high wall in a jail-break sketch.

The spirit of these moments was epitomized by Steve one evening when he remarked to his audience, "I wonder what plot they have against my life tonight?" And, considering the awkward and risky positions in which he often found himself, his question was legitimate.

Some of Steve's viewers wondered why he so frequently participated in comedy gambles that lesser men might have considered too dangerous to attempt. Steve was asked by a member of the audience if he did the Harold Lloyd-type antics because he wanted to or because he *had* to.

"I do them," Steve replied, "because I *have* to *want* to—and I *want* to *have* to. It comes out even all around. Actually the staff comes around to me about once a week and asks, 'Would you object to being shot out of a cannon?'—little things like that.

"I say yes, I would object, and then somehow they order the cannon anyway. Then once they've gone to all the expense to order these chicken feathers and whatever else they order for me—cannons and nets and alligators to wrestle with—it seems the decent thing to go *through* with it, so it shouldn't be a total loss, as the saying goes. *I* may be a total loss some night, but at least we won't waste the equipment."

Among the more dangerous stunts in which Allen participated were the following: he was attacked by ten giant, live tarantulas, another time swarmed over by hundreds of vicious, large red ants. He was blown up—by actual dynamite—in a trunk; driven at sixty miles an hour into a solid wall of ice; dangled from a tightwire; swung on a high, circus trapeze bar; walked into a screened cage full of thousands of bees; hurtled down a fire escape chute from a five-story building; set on fire while wearing asbestos clothes; growled at by assorted wild beasts, and —to top it all off—went walking in midair on the upper wing of a 1916 stunt plane, the same plane made famous in the motion picture *It's a Mad, Mad, Mad, Mad, Mad World.*

The show's movie burlesques were also minor classics. "One night," Allen recalls, "we did a takeoff on the movie *The Longest Day.* We had La Mirada Avenue converted into a battleground—with trenches, machine guns, barbed wire, the works. At the climax, I gave the signal to attack, and all of our troops stormed the Hollywood Ranch Market, a grocery store across the street from the theater, bayoneting watermelons, throwing green peppers like grenades, and firing rifles. We really took the customers by surprise." This, of course, is a gross understatement; the Allen crew was a constant source of shock to shoppers and pedestrians in the vicinity.

Some of the slapstick games perpetrated by Allen and his crew in and around La Mirada Avenue finally palled on the permanent residents of that normally quiet residential street. After a few months of midget-car races, elephant parades, motorcycle invasions, and the like, a group of sixty-five residents complained formally to the Los Angeles City Council, citing obstruction hazards—scenery, furniture, cables, floodlights, sandbags, animals in cages, paint, tools, baggage, etc.—blocking the street. Miss Cecil J. Lewis, leader of the complainers, asked, "How would you like to go into your backyard and find Steve Allen sitting up in a tree, and a chimpanzee picking blossoms in your flower garden?"

Steve's reaction was, "Can I help it if they happened to send us a chimp that likes flowers? If that lady wants to even matters up, I hereby give her permission to come to our house and climb one of our trees."

Allen continued the inventiveness that had, a decade earlier, made the *Tonight* show so popular. For example, one evening he conducted an experiment designed to discover just how many viewers really paid attention to the portion of the ninety-minute-nightly comedy program devoted to the announcement of guests.

"It's been my theory that nobody ever really hears what our announcer Johnny Jacobs is shouting over the opening theme of the show," Steve stated, "so we decided to devise a method of finding out just how many people actually pay attention to what is said. To this end we recently substituted some absolute gibberish for the announcement of guests normally given at the start of the program, and for two nights in a row Johnny Jacobs shouted these words at the beginning of the show: 'From Hollywood it's the Steve Allen Show . . . featuring the ferman of Dorm Kravemen and his habbiddee, the klam of George Peeven and his loll, and direct from three straight clydes at the Zip Raggan Room, the fabulous Klermans. And now he he is—the fane of our pin—Steve Allen.'"

And what was the result of Steve's experiment?

"We didn't receive a single letter or phone call from anyone asking just what it was Johnny said. From this we assume that people either really *believed* that our guests included the ferman of Dorm Kravemen or that, as I'd predicted, no one really pays attention to the announcements made at the beginning of television programs."

Critical reaction to the Steve Allen Westinghouse program was predictably enthusiastic. Many of the reviews

opened with an expression of pleasure at Allen's return
to late-night television after a long absence.

"Allen's hand has never lost its skill," observed the reviewer for *Los Angeles* magazine, "nor his wit its celerity.
And, as good as his prime time network shows were, the
evidence is now overwhelming that Allen is at his best
in the fey and fading hours of the night.

"In curious ways, the new show seems an improvement
over the old and glorious *Tonight* show. Nobody seems
to be listening tautly for the sound of distant drummers,
but only doing and enjoying what comes naturally . . .
the last lingering doubters are now persuaded, along
with the rest of us, that no one can interview studio audiences so deftly, extracting so much humor at no cost (that
is, humiliation) to the interviewees. Program guests now
run heavily to the oddballs—the woman who plays musical combs, the man devoutly convinced that shaking
hands upsets psychic balances, the nature boy who finds
strength through herbs.

"The show is long on Allen's particular brand of comic
inventiveness. One evening, having found two look-
alikes for himself, he led the cameras on a frantic chase
around the studio, seeming to be in three places at once.

"The shows are not necessarily released in the order
in which they are taped. As a result, one evening Allen
had the pleasure of introducing Terry Gibbs as 'the man
who did such a great job on tomorrow night's show.'"

A simple device that developed into one of the most
potent and popular intermittent events on the Westinghouse show was the "funny phone call." A name would
be picked at random from the phone book and Steve, in
talking with the respondent, would assume a variety of

vocal disguises or pretend to be in some odd predicament. One evening, for instance, calling an automobile club, he reported that his car had just gone over Malibu Canyon.

"You better watch that," said the auto club agent.

"I did," Steve said. "It was beautiful."

"Is there any reason," said the respondent, "why it has to be pulled out tonight?"

"Well," said Steve a little testily, "I've got to get home *somehow*." When the audience laughed, he explained, "Sorry. I'm calling from a saloon out in Malibu and these drunks are laughing at me."

Allen's analysis of the delight the audiences found in these phone calls gets to the root of the brand of humor involved: "They all appreciated that it was ad lib. Audiences can distinguish between spontaneous humor and the written joke. Besides, this gave them the sense of being in on something—you know, 'Aren't we devils, we're playing a practical joke on this poor guy who works for the automobile club.' It's a mildly sadistic factor. But if I had been rude to the man, or cruel, the laughter would have stopped immediately. You have to control yourself to the point where you never become smart-alecky or superior. As long as you can keep it within these boundaries, it remains a happy form of audience participation."

After two years of this sort of thing, CBS, Allen's original television employers, asked him to return to the network as master of ceremonies of the *I've Got a Secret* program, Garry Moore having temporarily retired from TV. Once Allen accepted this job he and Westinghouse agreed to separate. After a few more months the program was canceled, by mutual agreement, much to the disgust of a new generation of high schoolers, college students, and young adults, most of whom had been too young to watch the original *Tonight* program, but who had reacted enthusiastically to Allen's uninhibited routines.

The spread of Allenisms—words and phrases invented or popularized by Steve—had continued unabated during the Westinghouse years. "Smock, smockl," the cry of the wild bird, invaded high school and college campuses all over the country. These words, uttered in the form of a high, piercing cry, were among a series of quasi-double-talk neologisms perpetrated by Steve. Some of the others were "fern," "kreel," and, of course, "fink." The use of this last, with constantly comic implications, persisted long after the Westinghouse series ended.

Satire is too sophisticated a form of humor to form a general base for the work of the average comedian. For Steve Allen, whose humor seems to be less constructed than released, satire has been a natural outlet.

Steve once commented that the true humor in everyday life was represented by an incident that followed an announcement by Los Angeles radio station KPFK that it was planning to do a program about the John Birch Society. Immediately there was a great outpouring of anticipatory letters of protest. Some of these letters included the admonition "If you go ahead with this broadcast, we are not going to buy any of the products advertised on your station." The joker in this deck of mail was that KPFK is a noncommercial station.

Allen has never done a program of his own about the John Birch Society per se, but the reader will be reminded of the grim ways of extreme rightism when he examines the following script, written by Steve—with an assist by Buck Henry—for an appearance on the exceptionally hip (and since defunct) television series *That Was the Week That Was*. The satire here is penetratingly savage, yet its comic qualities were basic enough to give the sketch an appeal for any listener other than an extreme right-winger, for whom the shoe would have fit with unbearable snugness.

THE TRUE-BLUE AMERICAN

INTERVIEWER: With concern about Communism ever on the increase, many Americans are taking a more active role in political controversy. I would like to introduce a man who is devoting all his energies to rooting out subversive elements, let the chips fall where they may. Ladies and gentlemen, Mr. Robert Wretch. Good evening, Mr. Wretch, it's good to see you.

ALLEN: Good evening, sir. It's good to be seen.

INTERVIEWER: Mr. Wretch, you've written a number of books and pamphlets about the issue of subversion, haven't you?

ALLEN: Indeed I have, sir. I am the author of such widely read and fully documented booklets as "Is Your Unborn Baby a Communist?" "Are the Yellow Pages a Red Chinese Plot?" and "Sandy Koufax: a Dangerous Lefty."

INTERVIEWER: Do you support yourself on the proceeds from your writings?

ALLEN: Not entirely. I am also president and founder of several distinguished hate groups.

INTERVIEWER: Tell us about some of them.

ALLEN: Well, you know the National Association for Mental Health?

INTERVIEWER: Yes.

ALLEN: Well, since mental health is a Communist plot I've organized the National Association for Mental Illness.

INTERVIEWER: You say mental health is a Communist plot?

ALLEN: That's right. Psychiatry itself is a plot by the Communists.

INTERVIEWER: What do you think Communism is?

ALLEN: A plot by the Jews.

INTERVIEWER: And what do you think Judaism is?

ALLEN: A plot by the psychiatrists.

INTERVIEWER: And you said that psychiatry was—

ALLEN: A plot by the Commies. Now you're getting the idea.

INTERVIEWER: Sir, what would you say is the biggest Communist front organization in the country today?

ALLEN: I would say that the biggest Communist front in the country today is . . . the Communist party.

INTERVIEWER: The Communist party!

ALLEN: Certainly. It's just a cover-up for the *real* Commies.

INTERVIEWER: And who are the real Communists?

ALLEN: Dwight Eisenhower, Richard Nixon, Billy Graham, and the Beatles!

INTERVIEWER: The Beatles?

ALLEN: Certainly! Moscow is cleverly brainwashing our young people with hypnotic music. But I say it again, if a man admits to being a Communist, forget him. It's the characters who *deny* they're Commies that we have to keep our eye on. After all, half the members of the Communist party these days are FBI agents in disguise anyway. I tell you, the Communist party is a Communist plot to throw us off the track.

INTERVIEWER: Well, now, take me for example. I'm an anti-Communist.

ALLEN: I don't care *what* kind of a Communist you are. We've got a file on ya.

INTERVIEWER: What other evidence of Communist subversion do you find around us?

ALLEN: Well, they're poisoning us with Commie television programs.

INTERVIEWER: For instance?

ALLEN: *Flipper*. A good American family gets chummy with a fish, know what I mean?

INTERVIEWER: I'm not sure.

ALLEN: Well, why don't they stick with their own kind? That's the American way! Next step—fish ask for equal rights. They go to our schools. They already have their own schools of fish! . . . Would you like a dolphin to fool around with your sister? And television—movies—they're as bad as the books we read. Like *Fanny Hill*—it destroys your *mind*.

INTERVIEWER: What about *Candy*?

ALLEN: It destroys your *teeth*.

INTERVIEWER: In the area of foreign policy, what do you think of the French?

ALLEN: They're a bunch of *pinks*.

INTERVIEWER: What about the Chinese?

ALLEN: They're a bunch of Chinks. Pinks and Chinks are dirty finks! We have nothing to fear from the Chinese.

They're just bluffers. Six hundred and fifty million bluffers.

INTERVIEWER: What about their atom bomb?

ALLEN: They stole it from the Russians.

INTERVIEWER: Well, now, wait a minute. Just the other day on Radio Free Europe . . .

ALLEN: Radio Free Europe? *You* wait a minute! That's another Commie outfit. Why, I happen to have personal knowledge that those people actually do some of their broadcasts in *Russian!* It's time the American people woke up to what's going on! I say get the US out of the UN, get the UN out of the US and get your big head out of my key light!

INTERVIEWER: [*Stepping back a bit*] Oh, I'm sorry. Say, I hesitate to bring this up, but you're connected with the Minutemen, aren't you?

ALLEN: Indeed, sir.

INTERVIEWER: Then perhaps you can tell us about the arrest some time ago of one of the Minutemen leaders. You recall that he was arrested as a child molester.

ALLEN: That's right, he was. But we never held it against him.

INTERVIEWER: Why not?

ALLEN: Because he molested only left-wing children.

INTERVIEWER: In closing, Mr. Wretch, who would you suggest as a good leader for the American people?

ALLEN: Well, there's only one man I know of who hasn't taken sides with the bleeding-heart liberals, fuzzy-minded do-gooders, military muzzlers, pinks, punks, and perverts. A man who'll get my support if he chooses to run again.

INTERVIEWER: And who is that?

ALLEN: Attila, the Hun.
INTERVIEWER: I thought he was dead.
ALLEN: That shows how much you know.
INTERVIEWER: Thank you, and good night!

6

WORDS ABOUT MUSIC

Allen's involvement with music, and his attitude toward it, may be said to have a link with his feelings about humor.

Jazz and popular music are for him principally a source of personal gratification and a means of communication with his audiences rather than a necessity in making a living. There is also in much of his music, especially when he plays jazz, an essential strain of spontaneity that parallels the improvisational nature of most of his comedy.

Though he has great respect for the more cerebral members of the jazz community, and in fact has provided some of the avant-gardists with more air time through the years than any other national television figure, Steve finds a greater personal rapport with those musicians who represent a less pretentious and more fundamental approach to music; particularly, of course, those who are blessed with a sense of humor.

Terry Gibbs, the vibraphonist, has been admired for many years in jazz circles, not only as an artist, but also as a happy-go-lucky fellow whose glib, fast-talking personality, self-deprecatory ethnic Jewish humor and perennial *joie de vivre* are as well known as his musicianship. Not surprisingly, Gibbs became a good friend of Allen's some years ago. They have made many appearances together, in person and on the air.

Steve's facility for linking the worlds of humor and music has been reflected in a variety of ways. One idea that turned out to be a great popular success in at least three media—television, records, and the printed word—came about by chance when a friend of his, a guitarist, told Steve about the answer his six-year-old son had given to a stock question, "Well, son, what did you study at school today?"

"Oh, nothing much," the youngster replied. "We learned about some cat named George Washington."

Evidently the boy had heard enough of this kind of talk around the house to assume it was standard English. The idea occurred to Allen that there would be a delightful contrast between the ultrasophistication of the hip musician's jive talk and the essential naïveté of the traditional fairy tale or children's story. This reflection promptly gave birth to the first of what turned out to be a series, which Allen called, with due reference to Aesop, *Bebop's Fables*. The stories were only a few hundred words long and took perhaps a half hour each to write. They were recorded by Steve in a Coral album and formed the basis for a small book containing four of the stories and published under the title *Bop Fables*.

The following example—slightly revised and updated—gives an idea of Steve's true ear for the nuances (often grossly distorted by squares) of this highly specialized conversational idiom.

THE THREE LITTLE PIGS

Once upon a time, in the land of Nitty Gritty, there lived three little pigs. One of the little pigs was very cool, another was more on the commercial side, and the third was, beyond the shadow of a doubt, as square as they come. In fact, he was almost octagonal.

One day as the three little pigs were taking five one of them chanced to pick up a copy of *Down Beat*.

"Say, fellas," he said, "I see here where the big bad wolf is playing a one-nighter in this area next week."

"Oh-oh," said the second little pig. "That means it's panic-time."

"This," said the square little pig, "is the most depressing news since Ronnie Reagan got out of show business."

"Right," said the hip little pig. "We'd better scuffle."

Since the approach of the big bad wolf indeed signaled danger, the three little pigs immediately set about the business of constructing suitable shelter.

The square little pig arranged a quick GI loan and in no time erected a sturdy Orange County modern bungalow, complete with wall-to-wall floors and a TV antenna.

The commercial little pig moved into a foreclosed condominium, and at the last possible moment the cool little pig built himself a small A-frame temple out of clarinet reeds and Scotch tape.

Well, children, the big bad wolf eventually arrived in town and the first place he went was to the home of the third little pig. Applying his hairy knuckles to the door he laid down a crisp paradiddle and said, "Man, it's a raid!"

"Pops," whispered the pig from behind the locked door, "it's after closing."

"Don't hand me that jazz," said the wolf impatiently. "Open up!"

"Sorry, Irv," said the pig. "You gotta make reservations. Besides, you shouldn't even be out this late. Ain't you hip to the curfew?"

"The what?" said the wolf.

"Curfew," said the pig.

"*Gezundheidt,*" said the wolf, hoping to pass as a television comedian.

"Fun-nee," said the pig. "I'll see you next week, same time, same channel."

"Charlie," said the wolf, with ill-concealed displeasure, "if you don't open that door I'll huff and I'll puff and I'll blow your house down."

"Tell me one thing," said the little pig. "What condition is your lip in?"

Enraged at this impertinence, the wolf came on like Joshua, the walls came tumbling down, and in no time at all the poor little pig was really gone.

The following day the big bad wolf traveled across town and knocked at the door of the second little pig.

"Who dat?" said the pig, trying to sound hip.

"Never mind," snapped the wolf, anxious for destiny to resume its inexorable march. "Open that door and gimme some skin, pig. Or gimme some pigskin, as the case may be."

"I'll handle the jokes," said the pig. "Did you have an appointment?"

"Don't bug me, buster," said the wolf. "When I'm in town I always stop at the Pork Club. Now open up!"

"No, man," said the pig. "In fact, not by the hair on my chinny-chin-chin."

"Well, what do you know about that," said the wolf. "That must be Sam, the Sham, in there!"

"Never mind the whisker jokes," said the pig. "I ain't gonna open up."

"Tell you what, baby," said the wolf with wily warmth, "I'll just peek through your keyhole."

"In a pig's eye you will," said the little pig, which angered the wolf so terribly that he huffed and he puffed and he blew the house down.

In a very short time the second little pig met the fate that had befallen his unlucky friend.

The next day the big bad wolf went to the home of the cool little pig and knocked on the door.

"Have no fear," he said, "Murray-the-K is here."

"I don't care if it's Paul Krassner," said the little pig. "Hang tough."

"Now, wait a minute," said the wolf, pretending not to have heard the rebuff. "I understand there's a session going on here today."

"Cut out, whitey," said the pig. "We are not televising the hearings."

"But I heard I could get my kicks here," said the wolf, "I'd like to sit in."

"I'm hip," said the little pig, "and if you'll just slide down the chimney, as per instructions in the script, I'll really give you something to sit in."

"Are you putting me on?" said the wolf.

"Well, yes and no," said the pig.

"Aw, man," the wolf said, sniffing at a wisp of smoke, "you wouldn't be lighting up in there, would you?"

"See for yourself, pops," said the pig.

Losing his patience at last, the wolf hitched up his mod strides, leaped to the roof, and in so doing dislodged a brick, which fell down the chimney and clanged loudly against the great iron pot in the fireplace.

"What was that?" the wolf shouted.

"E flat," said the pig. "Daddy, fall in."

And fall in the wolf did, down the chimney and right into the pot. Nimbly, the little pig clapped a cover on the top and the wolf was trapped.

"Let me out," he howled. But the little pig was merciless. "Burn, baby, burn," he replied.

After allowing the water to simmer for forty-eight hours over a low flame, the little pig lifted the cover and peered down into the pot, sniffing tentatively.

"Ah," he said, with a broad smile, "my favorite soup. Cream of Nowhere."

* * *

It is interesting that back in his high school days, when Allen first broke into print as a humorist by submitting assorted jokes and light verse to the Chicago *Tribune*, he also submitted to *Down Beat* a brief article making fun of band leaders' slogans, which that magazine printed. Starting from such actual examples as "Swing and Sway with Sammy Kaye," the seventeen-year-old Allen went on to suggest:

> Swing Your Dames to Harry James
> Boopa-Doopa with Gene Krupa
> Just Go Crazy with Count Basie
> Fall Down to Les Brown
> Tonight Surprise 'er with Kay Kayser
> Start a Fight with Horace Heidt

He considered, but did not submit:

> Come on, you Bastar's, It's Frankie Masters

To the present moment Allen continues to be fascinated by orchestra billings, and every once in a while will dream up a name for a mythical combo along similar lines. A few recent instances:

> Sam Brown and His Belters
> Harley Davidson and His Three Cylinders
> Junior Hadassah and His Orchestra
> Davey Jones and His Full Fathom Five
> Dalton Trumbo and The Unfriendly Ten
> Dr. Ralph and His Bunche
> "Twas" Brillig and the Slithy Toves
> Judeo Christian and His Mambo Rhythms
> Earl Warren and the Justices
> Dow Jones and the Industrials

Steve is also an expert at naming vocal groups, such as The Strep Throats, The Dropouts, The Hangups, and a quartet called Three Jews and a Goy.

Occasionally these inventions must be classified as strictly inside jokes. For example, taking Fat Jack Leonard and Whispering Jack Smith as a point of departure, he wanted to introduce a friend named "Tacit" Al Fine. "If that doesn't mean a thing to you," he added, "don't worry—unless you are a musician, it shouldn't."

Allen also conceived the story of the two hipsters who started to drive from New York City to Los Angeles. "Have you got the road map?" said the first. The second replied, "No, man. But I brought along a copy of 'Route 66.'"

* * *

JAZZ MASS AT ST. PAUL'S

News item: Norwalk, Conn.—Jazz resounded through the vaults of St. Paul's Church today, celebrating "The Twentieth-century Mass" with the aid of a four-man jazz combo. The Reverend Anthony P. Treasure, rector, called the service "very reverent, very impressive, very moving." In his sermon Father Treasure made no direct allusion to his innovation, but spoke on the theme "God is not only, or primarily, interested in religion," a quotation from an unnamed Dean of Canterbury.

> Saturday night we went to confession
> And Sunday we had a crazy session
> When the Reverend Anthony P. Treasure
> (With a steady four beats to the measure)
> Said, "Welcome to our Sunday school
> And I'm sure you'll find it very cool."
>
> To tell the truth I dug his sermon.
> The man came on like Woody Herman
> And, dad, it was a real gas
> When the choir sang "How High the Mass."
> You could tell he was a swingin' gate
> The way he passed the collection plate;
> But the brethren almost blew their tops
> When the acolytes called the Reverend "Pops."
>
> Instead of *"Ite, missa est"*
> He feels that "Go, man, go!" is best

While Paul's Epistle to the Jews
He reads to the St. Louis Blues
Played by a wailing alto sax
So hip the ushers flip their stacks.
The group's so wild they ought to disc 'em.
(Who said "Fats Domino Vobiscum?")

Now I don't want to drag the scene
But let me lay down what I mean:
One goes to church to save one's soul,
Not to rock and not to roll
And, man, I doubt if good St. Paul
Would really dig this kind of ball.

Perhaps I may be somewhat square
When it comes to progressive prayer
But I suspect the Holy Ghost
Would not consider it the most,
And though the congregation cool it
A bishop still might overrule it
Or else someday when our souls fly
To that big Birdland in the Sky
We might hear Prez, or Bird, or Gerry
And an unnamed Dean of Canterbury
Tell Gabriel to lose his horn,
Get lost with his old-fashioned corn.
Imagination falters, faints
When it considers swinging saints
Led by Louis, Roy, or Bix,
Heard from the Jordan to the Styx.
So let's not sell the organ yet,
Despite the groovy press we get.

You have your horns and though you blow them
Still by their fruits, 'tis said, ye'll know them
So cool it for the moment, gate,
Or we might see this tragic fate:
Mass in the vernacular—
A Timex Jazz Spectacular.

THE DEATH OF THE BLUES
(A Parody)

Oh . . . they say some people long ago
Were searching for a corny lick,
Some commercial click
The dee-jays would pick.
First they destroyed a melody
And then they sang a bit off-key.
They didn't know just what to use
And that is how the blues
Really got sick!

They took the schmaltz
Of a waltz
And with all of its faults
Why, that led to
The Death of the Blues.

They took a note
From the throat
Of an old ferry boat
And that led to
The Death of the Blues.

From an old saloon
They took a tune, heard almost daily.
Even Dr. Spock
Suffers a shock, hearing Bill Haley.

They played the sax
On their backs,
Hit the drums with an axe
And I call that
The Death of the Blues.

II

They took the sound
Of a hound
Rollin' 'round on the ground
And I call that
The Death of the Blues.

They played too loud
But they bowed
To the crowd mighty proud
And that led to
The Death of the Blues.

From a kitchen clock
They took the tock,
Rocked it and rolled it.
Ran it in the ground,
Kicked it around,
But finally sold it.

They beat the tar
Every bar
Out of Presley's guitar
And that led to
The Death of the Blues.

That's the flop of the mop
In the old record shop
But I call it
The Death of the Blues.

THE DANCE BAND REMOTE

During his early KOY years, in addition to playing piano, singing, and spinning records, Allen spent some time announcing dance-band broadcasts from a local ball-room.

The conventional style of announcing these broadcasts was invariably a source of amusement to him. The ball-room from which one of these fifteen- or thirty-minute live remote shows emanated might be a three-floor walk-up next door to a garbage dump, yet it was part of the announcer's job to make it seem like the most glamorous place on earth. If it was located ten miles from the nearest transportation, it still had to be discussed as if it were no less accessible than one's own backyard.

For anyone who remembers the character of these broadcasts and the desperate efforts of the announcers to kill time when the musicians were setting up their parts for the next number, Steve's imaginary radio remotes, the first of which he wrote in college, are still among the

funniest and most nostalgic of all his routines. Here is
a typical example:

(MUSIC: HOTEL-STYLE ARRANGEMENT)
(CAMERA: BALLROOM BAND, SINGERS SEATED, OLD-
FASHIONED FLOOR MIKE DOWNSTAGE. SKITCH HENDERSON AT
PIANO. STEVE, TIGHT TUX, SLICK HAIR)

STEVE:

Good evening, ladies and gentlemen out there along the
radio airwaves. From the beautiful Aragon Ballroom, high
atop the fabulous Hotel Fabulous, in the heart of downtown Gallup, New Mexico, just a short forty-five-minute
drive from the ball-bearing center of the world, Leaven-
worth, Kansas, the National Broadcasing Company is
sending your way the rancid rhythms of Scratch Humper-
dink and his Makes-You-Want-to-Call-the-Cops Music.
Yes, direct from the stunning new Laundry Room of the
glamorous Hotel John Dillinger, a refreshing two and
one-half-mile swim across Lake Michigan, just underneath
the heart of downtown Birmingham, Alabama, where
the Ohio River meets the Panama Canal to form the St.
Lawrence Seaway, it's the sticky fingers of old Skeets
Horsefeathers, the Tom Swift of the Piano, with another
seventeen solid hours of danceable, pranceable, horrible
melodies on your radio. And now, Stump Hatchethead
and his midgets ask the musical question: Who?

(MUSIC: BAND PLAYS)

STEVE:

Thank you, Slimy, that was sickening. Friends, in case
you're just joining our jamboree, the Mutual Bumrushing

Company is heaving your way the hair-curling selections of Splash Hackenbush and his Twelve Angry Men, direct from the brand-new Locker Room of the beautiful Hotel Eichmann, a short haul from the mouth-watering fig fields of the 1934 Mississippi State Fair Grounds on the banks of the Amazon River just across from the Pearl of the Orient, Paramus, New Jersey. Now, Scrooge Hupmobile and his Teen-age Gorillas get together as our swooning, crooning vocalist, Rock Garden, offers this lyrical advice. Rock?

(MUSIC: BAND PLAYS. BOY SINGS)

STEVE:

Ah, yes, isn't he wonderful, and girls, he's available, because he's just been fired. Friends, in case you're just tuning in, the Crumbling Block-busting System is unloading its musical trash basket right into your living rooms, presenting the brain-numbing selections of Studs Hangover and his All-Washed-up Orchestra direct from the breath-taking new Men's Room on the seventy-sixth floor of the Hotel Adolph Hitler, on the outskirts of Los Alamos, New Mexico, just a thrilling ten-second rocket flight from the chicken-plucking center of the great Northwest, Capetown, South Africa. So turn up your radio, roll up the rugs, and plug up your ears, and listen to that lovely little lady of song, Jaynie Ferman as she recalls, "These Foolish Things."

(MUSIC: GIRL'S SONG)

STEVE:

Ah, yes, isn't she lovely? Friends, if you're tuning in late, the American Back-breaking System is shoving down your throats the sweetest music this side of Sodom and Gomor-rah, played by the old Pinhead of the Piano, Shucks Hemoglobin and his Lawrence Welk Rejects, direct from the freshly repainted Broom Closet of Frank Daily's Meadowbrook, high atop the recently built Hotel Jayne Mansfield, directly across the river from downtown Levit-town, the date-nut bread center of the world. Yes, it's the regular musical massacre by the old King Kong of the Keyboard, Schmaltz Hickerynut, and his Misguided Mis-siles, coming to you from the lovely Interrogation Room of the David Susskind Hotel, just a hop, skip, and a jump from the International Cotton-picking Festival in the heart of the Nation's Quicksand Center, Batista, Ohio.

Now friends, the old clock on the wall says our Saturday Night Dancing Party is on its last legs, so until next time, this is your announcer, Clem Cryle, saying toodle-oo, a bit of a tweet-tweet, a fond adieu, a *yock-she-mosh*, a bit of a pip-pip, a punch in the mouth, pleasant dreams, an *au revoir*, an *auf Wiederzsehen*, good night, good-bye, lots of health, lots of fun, and lotsa luck. This is NBC, the National Brainwashing Company.

(MUSIC: UP TO PLAYOFF)

PRACTICAL JOKES

Of all the effects of Steve Allen's sense of humor on his relationship to the world of music, the most hilarious and probably the most celebrated is the Buck Hammer in-cident.

In 1959 Allen was a partner in a recording company, Hanover-Signature Records. Since he had complete freedom to record anything he liked, and somewhat less than complete faith in the ear of the average music critic, he decided to play a practical joke in the form of a recording session.

He invented a Negro pianist named Buck Hammer, whose life story was not unlike that of the late Meade Lux Lewis. As all jazz fans know, Lewis had been rediscovered in the 1930s, washing cars in a Chicago garage, after years of obscurity. John Hammond, his discoverer, promptly arranged a record date for him and through Lewis the whole boogie-woogie piano craze was established.

Steve concocted a vaguely similar story for the liner notes on the Buck Hammer album. The piano music in the album was played, of course, by Steve himself; on a couple of tracks there was even some overdubbing, with Allen playing two piano parts.

Needless to say, the gag worked beautifully in both the lay and the trade press. The following review appeared in the *New York World Telegram:*

> *The Discovery of Buck Hammer,* Buck Hammer (Hanover). This will be Mr. Hammer's first and last album (his recent death was a tragic loss). Buck was a boogie-woogie piano player who could hold his own with such top men as Pete Johnson, Albert Ammonds and Meade Lux Lewis. Buck felt his music and attacked a selection with verve and depth. The fare is all originals, or such original adaptations as " 'Tenderly' Boogie" and " 'Tea for Two' Boogie." A great album.

But the greatest source of surprise to Steve was that he even fooled *Down Beat*. The following review, written by George Hoefer, appeared in the October 29, 1959, issue of the "Musicians' Bible."

Buck Hammer

THE DISCOVERY OF BUCK HAMMER—Hanover HM-8001: *Blue's Blues; Hackensack Train; Jungle Boogie; Frank's Blues; Ridiculous Boogie; Golly Gee Boogie; Fink's Mules; Minor Boogie; Tenderly Boogie; Practice Boogie; Too Fast Boogie; Tea for Two Boogie.*

Personnel: Buck Hammer, piano with unknown drummer and bongos.

RATING: * * *

Boogie Woogie piano may have the gone the way of ragtime to become an obsolete musical idiom, but here we hear an unusual pianist, now dead, who came out of the woods in 1956 and made some records in Nashville, Tenn.

Buck Hammer apparently suffered from the same personal shrinking-violet malady that bothered several other piano players, including Peck Kelly, Jack (Obie) O'Brien, and Joe Abernathy, all of whom refused to present themselves to a wider public than their immediate friends.

Hammer, from Glen Springs, Ala., was nowhere near the boogie woogie artist that Meade Lux Lewis, Albert Ammons, Pete Johnson, or even Pine Top Smith proved to be. But as a blues pianist, he was more creative than any of these men.

All numbers in this set are Hammer originals, excluding Walter Gross' *Tenderly* and the Youmans-Caesar *Tea for Two*. He performs these two in a half boogie, half Latin style.

Hammer plays with both hands and has the elements of a vital blues attack in either of them. His left hand is in full display in *Blue's Blues* and *Too Fast Boogie*. One of the most interesting tunes is *Practice Boogie,* where Hammer uses his left hand to build a bass pattern from a child's piano exercise and then, with his right, does practice figures to fill in.

This is a worthwhile addition to a jazz piano library as an example of an unusual basic-blues pianist, who deigned, at the request of his brother, to make one trip to Nashville to put some of his originality on record for posterity.

There would certainly have been many more such adulatory reviews, but unfortunately the secret of Buck Hammer did not last long. The story was exposed in *Time;* but this was not the end of the Hammer saga. The late Ed Sherman, who wrote a humorous column for *Down Beat* under the name of George Crater, announced that Ira Gitler, another jazz critic, was planning to write Buck Hammer's autobiography, *His Eye Is on the Shot Glass.* Sherman followed this announcement with a series of personal reminiscences about Hammer. Steve, deciding to carry the gag just one step further before Hammer returned to obscurity, reacted as follows:

January
Seventeenth
1960

Mr. Ed Sherman
Fairfax Inc.
270 Madison Avenue
New York 16, New York

Dear Ed:

Thanks very much for your wonderful story about me in the February 4 issue of DOWNBEAT.

When a man has worked as long as I have for recognition, it is really great that people like yourself are helping me to achieve the acclaim that I deserve. There was just one little mistake in your story, by the way . . . I *do* have three hands. In fact, *that* is the reason I have always been so shy about playing in the big cities, going on TV and the like.

Down here people accept me for what I am and I am in great demand for games of three-handed poker, wild necking and the like.

As you have no doubt dug, that part about me dying was also an ofay lie.

I think the way it got started was that when a cat from New York interviewed me, I said I'd rather die than play the Metropole.

Watch your step,
Buck Hammer

To pull off successfully, even once, a stunt on the order of the Buck Hammer affair was a rare coup; but Allen, hungry for blood—or really for fun—decided a few months later to try it again. The next creature of his imagination was Maryanne Jackson. Steve cut an album of piano solos with rhythm accompaniment, this time satirizing certain ultramodern piano trends in much the same way Buck Hammer had parodied boogie-woogie. He included all kinds of patently absurd harmonic changes and utterly meaningless random notes, but instructed his rhythm section to play normally.

He wrote a set of highly imaginative liner notes about

Miss Jackson, then compounded the fiction by asking his housekeeper, Mary Sears, to dress up in an evening gown and having her photographed at the piano in the Allen living room.

This time he scored an even more remarkable knockdown. *Jazz Review*, a short-lived intellectual magazine well known for its hipper-than-thou attitude, swallowed the story hook, line, and clinker. A highly critical analysis appeared, written as if the reviewer were puzzled by Miss Jackson's musical approach but felt it worthy of serious, scholarly study.

To round off this incident as he had closed the other, Steve dictated a letter, which his secretary, Donna Zink, wrote in longhand on ladylike blue stationery. The letter was addressed to the *Jazz Review* critic and was signed by Maryanne Jackson. Sure enough, *Jazz Review* took the letter at face value and printed it. This particular flight of fancy was never exposed, so if the editors of *Jazz Review* read this book it will be news to them.

The object of the Buck Hammer and Maryanne Jackson ruses was probably Steve's desire to prove to himself that you can fool some of the people all of the time. Had the first incident not been exposed, then he and his fellow musicians would have been the only ones to relish the private humor of the episode.

Another example of the fun Allen derives from music, similarly private in nature and never revealed to this day, began one evening in my living room. Bob Bach, producer of *What's My Line?*, happened to mention that some song titles might present impossible challenges to lyricists. His example: "Faggots and Dykes." "For the next hour or so," he recalls, "while the rest of us were en-

gaged in frivolous conversation, Steve was quietly at
work jotting down some lines of verse.

"Finally he rose and told us he had conceived an idea
for a song. He then played and sang it for us. It was a
moving, melodramatic tale set in the Netherlands, where,
in the winter, when the dikes are almost overflowing,
hardy Dutch citizens go out at night with flaming flares
and fagots to guide their sailors home. Steve even had
sheet music of the song printed and handed out copies to
a few friends, until his frantic manager had them all im-
pounded for fear of damage to the public Allen image.
The song, oddly enough, was perfectly clean. Only the
title was an eyebrow-raiser."

7

WORDS ABOUT NAMES

Because he has always had a self-analytical way with words and has a lively interest in etymology, semantics, and related studies, Allen's antennae are always sensitive to terminological and appellative curiosities. As a consequence a number of his sketches, as well as many of his ad-lib remarks both offstage and on, have been concerned with odd names he has devised for people, places, and objects.

Ever since the earliest days of Tab Hunter and Rock Hudson, for instance, he has been fascinated by the concept of pithy names for movie stars. He invented Candy Bar long before a lady using an almost identical name actually made her bow in the cabarets. Rip Torn is not, though in all justice he should have been, a creature of the Allen mind; but Steve can take credit for Tab Collar, Race Riot, Hub Cap, Stark Naked, Gear Shift, Zip Code, Punch Board, Flash Flood, Crash Helmet, Sistine Chapel, Chuck Steak, and Rock Pyle.

He has such mythical and delightful friends as Truman Kaput, George W. Shibboleth, Gregg Shorthand, the celebrated female politician Goldie Bearwater, and the noted French actress Yvette Peignoir. He has also referred to the two celebrated Russian authors Pushkin and Pullkin.

He once reeled off a logical sequence of Greek philosophers: Socrates, Plato, Homer, and Jethro. He claims his dentist once told him he was suffering from a peculiar condition known as oral roberts; it is brought on by watching television with the mouth open.

Even the names of actual people sometimes hold a weird attraction for him. Once on his Westinghouse show, after presenting a girl singer named Philly Duke, he pointed out that this must surely be a brand of cigar, then advised the audience, "Smoke a Philly Duke, friends."

He is very strong on gangsters' names. On one occasion he remarked, "See that man sitting at the table over there? That's Maxie Copacabana. He owns the Trocadero. The fellow across from him is Tony Trocadero. He runs the Copacabana."

Once he started a "menu gang," composed of such characters as:

> The headman, Mr. Big: "Oysters" Rockefeller
> The muscleman: "Beef" Stroganoff
> The moll: "Cherries" Jubilee
> The stool pigeon: "Chicken" Cacciatore
> An old-time gambler: "Potatoes" O'Brien
> A waterfront boss: "Clams" Marinara
> A small-time hood: "Frog Legs" Sauté
> A one-time big operator: "Eggs" Benedict
> A safe-cracker: "Soup" du Jour
> Mafia rep: "Veal" Scallopini
> A lookout: "Shrimp" Cantonese

Allen also would be a handy man for foreign automobile manufacturers to turn to when they run short of names for their sports models. He swears that he once traded in his 1954 Sunbeam-Mixmaster for a 1959 Fiasco. He more recently bought an Italian roadster, an Alfalfa-Farina, a car he says is very popular with the Our Gang crowd. He hopes soon either to buy a low-slung 1966 Magna Carta or a rebuilt 1954 Taft-Hartley.

His inventions even include inventors: he claims to have once introduced Charles W. Stilson, inventor of the Stilson Wrench, to Irving P. Monkey, inventor of the Monkey Wrench.

He has also created his own street intersections ("I met her at the corner of Gower and Champion"), his own imaginary menu item for New York's glamorous Forum restaurant (Pair of Belgian Hares in Flagrante Delicto, $19.50), and a real estate development ("Folks, take advantage of the fine real estate opportunities in that fast-growing community, Ground Zero, California").

Pharmacists may be interested to know that he has invented a tranquilizer that fizzes, Trauma-Seltzer; also a combination hangover and cold medicine, half methedrine and half anahist, which, naturally, he calls Methodist.

Asked the names of the Schubert brothers, he said, "Let's see. Lee Schubert, Jake Schubert, Pineapple Schubert, Strawberry Schubert, Orange, Lemon, and Lime."

One of Allen's best-known gambits with names is the attachment of ironically appropriate authors' by-lines to actual well-known books of which, however, they were not the real authors.

They include the following:

1. *The Man in the Gray Flannel Suit*—by Gen. Robert E. Lee

2. *You Can't Go Home Again*—by Juan Perón
3. *Of Time and the River*—by Willie Sutton
4. *Something of Value*—by Bobo Rockefeller
5. *Love Is a Many-Splendored Thing*—by Tommy Manville
6. *The Bad Seed*—by Luther Burbank
7. *Wish You Were Here*—by Judge Crater
8. *Lady in the Dark*—by Mrs. Tom Edison
9. *The Wapshot Chronicle*—by Frank Costello
10. *Some Came Running*—by Willie Shoemaker
11. *The Organization Man*—by Carmine De Sapio
12. *Don't Go Near the Water*—by Joe E. Lewis
13. *A Man Called Peter*—by Mary Healy
14. *The Day the Money Stopped*—by Bobby Baker
15. *Bus Stop*—by Mike Quill
16. *The Last Angry Man*—by Gov. Wallace
17. *Where Did You Go? Out. What Did You Do? Nothing*—by Sen. James Eastland
18. *Life Plus 99 Years*—by Jack Benny
19. *Naked to Mine Enemies*—by Brigitte Bardot
20. *Ice Palace*—by C. P. Snow
21. *Good-bye, Mr. Chips*—by Nick, the Greek
22. *I Led Three Lives*—by The Maguire Sisters
23. *A View from the Bridge*—by Steve Brodie
24. *There's No Business Like Show Business*—by John Wilkes Booth
25. *How I Turned One Thousand Dollars into One Million in Real Estate in My Spare Time*—by Fidel Castro
26. *Listen, Yankee*—by Casey Stengel
27. *Growing Up Absurd*—by Beverly Adland
28. *Please Don't Eat the Daisies*—by Gaylord Hauser

29. *14 for Tonight*—by Frank Sinatra
30. *The Shirt Off My Back*—by Marlon Brando
31. *Come On'a My House*—by Conrad Hilton
32. *Call Me Madam*—by Polly Adler
33. *We Three*—by John Charles Thomas
34. *For Whom the Bell Tolls*—by Dr. Frances Horwich
35. *The Sea Around Us*—by Lloyd Bridges
36. *Candy*—by Robert Welch
37. *One Potato, Two Potato*—by Spud Murphy

Steve's faculty for attaching hilariously appropriate names to fictional characters is perhaps best demonstrated in one of his shortest short stories, an Allen's eye view of Greek mythology.

* * *

MYTHOLOGY SIMPLIFIED

Onus, the greatest of all the gods, and his faithful spouse, Stigma, lived peacefully for many centuries high atop Mount Ipana. They had issue from time to time, and three of their sons, Virus, Peruna, and Epidermis, decided to visit the earth below to see if the maidens of Greece were as fair of face and figure as rumor would indicate. Pumice, however, the god of Finger-stain, was very jealous when he heard about their proposed jaunt, and he sent Fulcrum, the god of Balance, to harass the three on their trip to earth. Virus, learning of Pumice's treachery, enlisted the aid of Monotony, the goddess of Inertia, and when the cards were down she did not fail him. Thundering across the heavens on her mighty steed, Pantages, she attacked Pumice's stronghold, and despite the efforts of

Plethora, the goddess of Oversupply, she routed the evil-doer and all his forces.

Returning homeward, unfortunately, she was set upon by Thermos and Pastrami, the gods of Hot Lunch, her horse Pantages was driven off, and she was banished to the island of Hypotenuse.

When Onus learned of this his anger knew no bounds. He at once sent for Parenthesis, the goddess of Bowed-legs, and ordered her to worm her way into the confidence of Thermos and Pastrami. Parenthesis was willing enough, but first, she announced, she would like to have Onus call back from the dead her two former husbands, Papyrus, god of Race-results, and Thesis, god of Graduation.

Onus granted her request and she forthwith set off on her assignment. Hearing that she was coming, Apathy, the god of Boredom, disguised himself as her former steward Digitalis, god of Revival, and told her that Thermos and Pastrami would welcome her with open arms.

Parenthesis, falling into this trap, sent her faithful bodyguard Perimetre back home, and thus unprotected was attacked and killed. Antithesis, long-lost son of Onus, happened to be in the neighborhood at the time, however, and reported to his father what had happened. As I recall the story Onus didn't seem to care much, and that's about all there is to Greek mythology. Next time the subject comes up at a party you may conduct yourself as an authority.

8

BY-LINES

The humor of Steve Allen as presented in the previous chapters is composed for the most part of material created spontaneously and performed on the air, on records, or both. This chapter differs from its predecessors in two respects: everything in it was *written* by Allen and all of it was designed to be read rather than performed.

On this level one finds an Allen more composed, a little more reflective and sedate in his humor. Indeed, in many of the following pieces the humor is secondary, the primary objective being the establishment of a particular point, a historical recollection, or a social observation.

His remembrance, for example, of such things past is as wistfully nostalgic as it is implicitly comic. Similarly the essays on sports announcing and the brief "think pieces," some of which evidence a John Crosbyish approach to journalism, are as important for their proof of Allen's perceptiveness of things and thoughts around him as they are for their humorous overtones.

* * *

THERE, BUT FOR THE GRACE OF GOD, GOES HARRY TRUMAN

Fan-magazine biographers have sometimes made the flattering observation that, inasmuch as I have successfully turned my hand to a number of trades, I might, if I wished, do almost anything. Nothing could be further from the truth. All successful men arrive at their professional goals partly by the mere chance that they have not been accidentally and permanently sidetracked into a field for which they were not particularly well fitted.

My first job, for example, was as a clothing salesman, and I was an abysmal failure at it. It was the summer of 1939, I was seventeen, as tall as I am now, killing time till school started, and eager to prove my maturity. A search of the help-wanted ads in the Chicago papers, however, led me to concentrate on the "*Boy*-wanted" section, a fact which speaks for itself.

One advertisement caught my eye because it asked for a "neatly dressed" boy. This appealed to me because it suggested that, whatever the job, it would not involve heavy manual labor. The salary stipulated was fifteen dollars a week. Somehow the fact that I would have to work six full days to earn this amount did not seem important; I concentrated instead on the vision of fifteen dollar bills in my hand, and on the idea that a like amount would be mine every week during the summer.

Early one humid June morning I staggered out of bed, ate a hasty breakfast, put on a clean white shirt, and rode downtown coatless on the Halsted Street streetcar. By the time I arrived at the address given in the advertisement I was no longer a neatly dressed boy. The muggy Chicago weather had crumpled my collar, the top button had popped off the shirt, and my carefully stick-umed hair had begun to come unglued—a problem that still troubles me.

My meager confidence needed shoring up and it received it when I climbed the narrow staircase to the second-floor business office where interviews were being conducted. Among the thirty or so boys who were standing in line ahead of me only four or five were what the writer of the ad must have had in mind when he included the adjective "neatly dressed." I had mixed emotions as I took my place in the line: selfish gratification that I would be one of the few neatly dressed, and intense sympathy for all the others. Their shirts were either those worn by laborers or else cheap-looking sports shirts, although God knows the boys wearing them looked as if they had precious little time for sport. Their shoes were run-down, their trousers shabby, their faces already marked by poverty. The nation was just emerging from the Depression and although my people did not have much money we were certainly better off than the majority of families in Chicago.

My nervousness increased as I drew nearer to the head of the long line, which wound its way into a small office. When at last my turn came to be interviewed I was surprised when a man behind a counter simply looked at me for a moment and then said, "Can you start work Monday morning?"

"Yes," I said.

"All right," he said, handing me a card. "Here's the address. You start work at eight o'clock every morning. The Washington Shirt Company. Wear a clean shirt every day."

I thanked him and walked out, elated. I had a job! Landing that particular job for fifteen dollars a week was a bigger thrill than I experience today when a sponsor calls up and tells us that I am hired for fifteen *thousand* a week. The reason, of course, is that in television such occurrences are commonplace, whereas when you are seventeen and the world is fresh and new every unusual experience assumes enormous proportions.

The following Monday my mother and aunt clucked over me like two worried hens, as I bathed, dressed, combed my hair, counted my car fare to the penny again and again, and prepared to go off into the workaday world. Ten thousand times I assured my aunt that, yes, I had a clean handkerchief, told my mother that, yes, I had gone to the bathroom, that, yes, I had enough money in my pocket, that, yes, my nails were clean.

At last I was sitting on the streetcar, alone, on my own, and greatly excited. I was going to work in a men's clothing store, obviously as a salesman. "May I help you?" I muttered to myself, smiling at an imaginary customer. Suddenly it occurred to me that I knew nothing whatever about the sizes of shirts, shorts, slacks, and jackets, their materials, their prices, or indeed anything at all about them. I could tell you the batting average of practically every player on the White Sox or the Cubs, or I could write a song or poem, but I didn't even know what size underwear I wore. A fine haberdashery salesman I was going to be.

When I arrived at the store, however, I was immediately relieved of my fears. The shop manager, a short, energetic man, greeted me pleasantly but curtly and at once ushered me into a basement stockroom. "You can get the lay of the land working down here for a few days," he explained. "For example, here's a stack of boxes containing men's collars. They're sorta mixed up. I want you to open all the boxes and make sure that they're all in order according to size. Then if any of us fellows yell down the stairs and ask for a particular size collar or shirt or anything why you hustle around, get the stuff, and shoot it up to us. Got that?"

I assured him that I had, without entirely believing it myself. As instructed, I began to sort collars, the old-fashioned, stiff, detachable sort seldom worn any more. To my consternation I observed that every one of the first dozen or so collars I touched was left with a dirty black smudge on it. My hands, after the ride on the dusty street-car, were none too clean. I washed up but said nothing about the soiled collars. To this day they're probably still in stock, going gracefully out of style.

I worked in the stockroom all that day, occasionally meeting the salesmen, who would sneak down one at a time for a smoke. What dashing, devil-may-care fellows they seemed, glibly rattling off the names and sizes of shirts and socks and shorts, cracking racy jokes, cursing without guilt, smiling good-naturedly in my direction, and calling me "Slim" or "Kid." I wondered if I might ever dream of being one of them. As it turned out this dream was never fully realized.

The following morning I was given another duty: dusting off the counters and shelves upstairs. A promotion! I was up from my dank dungeon, up among the breezy salesmen. But not for long; when my dusting chores had been completed I was once again dispatched to the lower regions to soil collars and learn the stock.

Toward the end of the week, however, it was decided that I might try my hand at selling. Business was brisker on Friday and Saturday and an extra hand could be used. Standing stiffly by a tie counter waiting for the arrival of my first customer I felt ill-at-ease and clammy-handed. The procedure had all been explained to me by the manager and it seemed simple enough; no more complicated, say, than bull fighting or hitting a home run with the bases loaded. You simply helped the customer to select what he had, after all, only come in to buy in the first place, then you gently tried to get him to buy a little more, and when he had completed his purchase you made out a sales slip, took his money, performed some sort of mysterious transaction at the cash register, and then wrapped up his purchase. By the time I finally faced my first customer I was so nervous I was ready to add his underwear and collar size and wrap up the cash register.

You don't just lunge competitively at customers when they walk into your shop, incidentally, in the way that fishermen lunge for salmon in the Columbia River. The salesmen rotate in turns so that the more enterprising will not hog more than their share of the action. Consequently it inevitably came to be "Allen's turn." Although I realize now that the other salesmen could not have been less interested in my handling of my first customer it seemed at the time that all eyes were on me. I felt that at any minute someone might begin selling tickets in the street. "Right in here, folks. Watch the young goof from the South Side make his first sale. Will he fumble it? Will he rack up a big one? Come in and find out. Hurry, hurry, hurry!"

When at last the dreaded moment came I stood uneasily near the front door. Not too near, of course. You mustn't appear overanxious. The fish must swim to you before you hook him. After what seemed like an interminable wait an alarmingly prosperous-looking middle-aged man walked purposefully in. I moved forward shakily. My lips had parted to speak when I felt the manager's hand on my arm.

"I'll take this one," he whispered. It turned out that the fish that had approached us was so big, such an extremely juicy-looking prospect, that he was too good a catch to risk with me, a novice. Clearly he called for expert handling. I felt only intense relief.

It must have been half an hour later that my turn came around again. A young man came in and said he wanted to buy a pair of socks. "Thank God," I muttered to myself. Socks were a cinch to package. You just threw them in a small paper bag.

"What size?" I asked, cleverly. He told me and I led him to a rack on which were displayed socks of all sizes and colors. As he looked over the stock, making up his mind, I silently prayed that he would buy only one pair. A large purchase would require addition, something that I felt hardly up to in my rattled state. Unfortunately he dashed my hopes by buying *three* pairs of socks. The nerve of the man. I smiled pleasantly enough, however, tossed his purchase into a bag, and began to make out the sales slip.

"Here's the money," he said, putting it on the counter to the penny.

"Wait," I said, not at all prepared to handle the transaction on such simple terms, "this will just take a second."

"I don't want a slip," he said. "Just gimme the socks."

"I'm sorry, sir," I said, my voice breaking, "but I have to make out a slip."

He sighed and gave up. The socks were forty-nine cents a pair. A foolish figure if ever I had heard of one.

Why not fifty cents? Three fifties were a dollar and a half, quick and businesslike. But who could tell what the hell three times forty-nine was? In this muddled state of mind I decided against multiplication altogether and instead wrote down 49 three times and began adding it up, even counting, I'm afraid, on my fingers.

"I'm in a little bit of a hurry," the customer said apologetically, interrupting my train of thought and forcing me to begin my calculations over again. Somehow, what seemed like hours later, the transaction was completed and I retired gratefully to the end of the line to await my turn again. How attractive, then, seemed the dim, moist depths of the stockroom. What peace reigned in its quiet shadows. But here I was, like a bug unearthed from under a rock, compelled to remain in the terrible glare of daylight, forced now to direct my unwilling feet toward a succession of customers.

Today, twenty years later, I naturally cannot recall the faces of all the people that I served during the next few days, but certain individuals do stand out in my memory. There was the dear little old lady who took her sweet time dawdling over her selection of shirts and sundries, and who then, when I had told her the cost, suddenly acted very much in a hurry. "I'm in a rush," she said. "Please give me my package." A short time later the manager brought to my attention the fact that I had shortchanged the store some three dollars in making out the slip and I understood the reason for the old lady's quick departure. This incident and others like it served to teach me something important, and sad, about human nature.

Then there was the time I blushed when a young

woman came in and purchased from me three pairs of Jockey shorts.

And I will never forget all the incredibly clumsy packages I wrapped. There were knots created that summer that no sailor could ever name, many of which I'm sure had a magical way of snapping open just as the packages they presumably secured were being carried onto crowded trolleys. The streets of Chicago that summer must have been littered with socks, shorts, undershirts, and ties that I had wrapped with the finesse of an orangutan. I included my thumb in certain knots, the end of my tie in others. Once or twice my packages fell apart even before the customer had reached the front door of our shop.

But somehow with the passing of the weeks I polished off a few of the rough edges. My packages began making it all the way to the suburbs, I imagine, instead of falling apart while still in the Loop, and my errors in addition were eventually limited to the area of nickels instead of dollars. To give myself credit, I finally developed a fairly smooth counter-side manner. Had I been able to hire a serf to handle sales slips and package wrapping I might have turned into a top-notch salesman; of such stuff dreams are made.

Another incident from this period that still is clearly etched on my memory is a visit my Aunt Mag made to the store one afternoon, just to say hello and see me in action. I felt rather proud of my semiadult status as I stood chattering with her, and even introduced her to the manager, who assured her I had immense possibilities. As she prepared to return to her own job, that of bill collector for the American Railway Express Company, she leaned close so as not to be overheard.

"Stevie," she whispered, "your shirt tail is hanging out. Tuck it in."

All the salesmen were sharp characters, but one in particular stood out. A man of about forty, he had the genial manner of the supersalesman as well as the typically glib line of chatter. He did card tricks when business was slow, knew all the latest stories, and kept up the spirits of the whole staff. One of his favorite tricks was to "put on" customers who came in, to josh them in such a subtle way that they themselves were never aware of what he was doing, but, with sly winks, to let the other salesmen know that he was performing for their benefit.

I am afraid it will not seem particularly amusing in print, but one of his favorite jokes was to say in a loud, clear voice to a woman who had asked for shirts or shorts, "Certainly, madam. Any circumsize?"

Of course the woman would always respond by saying, "Yes, he takes a large, I think," or, "Well, he's about a thirty-eight," while the rest of us would bust a gut stifling giggles in the background.

One stunt Charley had perpetrated was regarded in the shop as a classic. Since it had taken place before my time I had to take everyone's word for it that the incident had actually happened as described.

A cloddish sort of lunk had come into the shop one day, according to the story, and had seemed like such a good target that Charley had pulled out all the stops.

"I wanna buy a slack suit," the mark had said.

"Certainly, sir," Charley had said. "Any circumsize?"

"Well, I don't know exactly. You better measure me."

"Very well, sir," Charley had said, pulling off a large sheet of wrapping paper about seven feet long and placing it on the floor. "Now, this type of slack suit is made according to a new tailoring principle so the sizes don't run the way they do with ordinary clothes. It'll be necessary for me, sir, to make an outline sketch of your entire body and that way we'll know exactly what size you take."

"What do you want me to do?" the outlander had said.

"Nothing to it at all, sir. You just lie right down on the floor on this piece of paper here and I'll draw the outline of your body with this Crayola."

The poor lug actually stretched out full-length on the floor while Charley measured him, all the while delivering a line of double-meaning patter for the benefit of the other salesmen who had gathered around. The others assured me the story was gospel, and, knowing Charley, I have no reason to doubt it.

THAT MAN TODAY IS BILL STERN

One day about five years after I had gone to New York and enjoyed various forms of good fortune I received a fan letter from a man in Los Angeles. "Congratulations on your success," he wrote. "I always knew you'd make it. You see, I remember you from the days when you started out, announcing the wrestling matches out here."

My correspondent erred in assuming that he had identified the moment of my professional debut, but he had nonetheless touched upon a phase of my career that has received no attention from the army of biographers who have swarmed through our offices during the past decade.

In the fall of 1949, while doing the KNX radio show, I received a call from an executive of the West Coast office of ABC Television. "We're thinking of trying something new with our wrestling matches out here," he explained. "We want somebody who can do a funny commentary on what's happening in the ring. We think you can do the job. What do you think?"

"It sounds like fun," I said. "Let's try it."

I didn't tell him that I knew nothing whatever about wrestling. In those days, as most readers will recall, the sport was a tremendously popular TV attraction and so I suppose it was automatically assumed that anybody with a TV set was an expert on the manly art. In any event I was given two weeks to prepare myself for the assignment, which I did by the simple expedient of watching the wrestling matches on station KTLA, which were announced by a fast-talking former actor named Dick Lane.

After watching Lane for three nights I came to the conclusion that, while he had profound knowledge of the fundamentals of wrestling, and could immediately identify standard holds such as the full nelson, the half nelson, the flying mare, and so forth, his names for other, more obscure positions came under the heading of creative writing. This insight I found greatly reassuring as the night of my first broadcast approached. The job, obviously, called for ad-libbing since, although it was rumored that a certain amount of rehearsals were involved in the game, I was not a party to them.

I arrived at the old Ocean Park Arena with a few wrestling jokes on cards, a pocketful of sharp pencils, and some notepaper.

By the time five minutes of the first match had gone by I had used up my meager supply of written jokes and was entirely on my own. Fortunately the first few holds were pretty Sears and Roebuck and I was able to glibly talk my way past them, but as the evening wore on the various chunky bodies that writhed and rolled before my vision began to get into positions that had never occurred to me and for which I had anticipated no terminology. I began to say any absurd thing I could think of, comforted by the knowledge that I was supposed, after all, to get laughs. If they had wanted a straight job of reporting they would have hired somebody else.

"Leone gives Smith a full nelson now," I said, "slipping it up from either a half nelson or an Ozzie Nelson. Now the boys go into a double pretzel bend with variations on a theme by Veloz and Yolanda. Now, Leone takes his man down to the mat! He has him pinned. Now they're rolling over. It's sort of a rolling pin."

Lest it seem peculiar that I can, at this late date, recall some of these jokes, I should explain that after every broadcast, and even during some of the filmed commercials, I would jot down my ad libs into a notebook, for I knew that during the coming weeks the opportunity to use some of them would present itself again.

The Ocean Park Arena in those days was a strange, noisy, animalistic place, with an atmosphere that I imagine was very close to that of the ancient Roman Coliseum. During every single minute of every match the air was rent with raucous cries, bloodthirsty lynch-mob imprecations, and general pandemonium, a fact that led me to conclude that people who frequent wrestling emporiums are not exactly our highest type of citizenry. Knowing that none of the people present could hear me I used to frequently comment on the bizarre characters who occupied the ringside seats.

"There's a man down there in the third row giving out with boo's and catcalls," I said one night, "and if I'd had that much booze I'd call a few cats myself. By the way, it's Ladies' Night here at Ocean Park, folks. There's still time to come on down, and you don't even have to prove you're a lady."

Comments of this sort, strangely enough, never received any criticism, but I got quite a few angry letters because of my jokes about wrestling itself. "If you think wrestling is so funny," was the general idea, "try getting into that ring yourself, wise guy." After a few weeks, however, the complaints stopped as the listeners got used to my unorthodox approach, and in due time they indicated that they heartily endorsed my jibes. "There's lots of cigar smoke in the air here," I said one night. "I don't like to say that this joint is *too* smoky but this is the only wrestling arena in town where they cure hams from the ceiling."

Actually those were the golden days of wrestling, at least in the financial sense. Wild characters like Gorgeous George, the human Air-Wick—and Baron Leone, who had the long, flowing tresses of a medieval philosopher—gave great color to the sport. When, at the end of the evening, I would beard these giants in their sweaty dressing room for some after-the-battle palaver I could never truly decide whether the animosity they displayed toward each other was real or faked, so heated were the performances. On more than one evening I found myself nervously separating two mammoths who seemed determined to continue their battle, even in the dressing room. After several months ABC decided to replace the matches with old movies, as I recall, but it was fun while it lasted and if things ever get tough I still have the gag file of wrestling jokes on hand.

Future historians perhaps will identify these contests as the first examples of rigged entertainment.

BASEBALL ANNOUNCERS

I was watching a baseball game on TV the other day and I noticed a peculiar thing. Years ago about all an announcer did was give you a play-by-play description of the game, but nowadays every time a player comes up to bat the announcer suddenly comes on like an encyclo- pedia and gives you a barrelful of statistics and folksy gossip. I'll show you what I mean.

All right, fans, Jones was the last man up for Los An- geles. He has now hit safely in seventeen straight games, his batting average is .321 and he took a good healthy swing at the ball, too, as he stood there wearing his size six- and seven-eighths baseball cap. Jimmy, as most of you fans probably know, is one of the seven players on the L.A. team who wear their socks inside out and, of course, it's all part of the game.

Klavenborn is the next man at bat. He's from East Bird- bath, Mississippi, a town that gave us several other great players, and he has now sprained his ankle in fourteen straight games, quite an impressive record.

Marty was injured early in the season. He had a slight

spike wound running from his left hip to his right knee-cap, but he's been playing a whale of a game lately and up to this afternoon he was one of the fourteen players in the major leagues who regularly refuse to take a shower after the game. He's coming out of the dugout and the crowd recognizes him by that peculiar little habit he has: chewing on the rosin bag. And now while Marty gets ready for the first pitch I just want to say a word to you men. Men, you owe it to your face to try the new Zip-master special razor. Notice how easily it works. *Zip,* it's open, *click,* it's loaded. *Mop,* it's empty. *Zam,* it's full. *Squish,* it's moistened. *Clang,* it's broken. *Wow,* it's fixed. *Bong,* it's sharpened. *Push,* it's tightened. *Pull,* it's loos-ened. *Plunk,* it's twisted. *Crack,* it's straightened. *Swunk,* it's dirty. *Swish,* it's cleaned. *Zoom,* it's shaving. *Scrape,* you're bleeding. It's as simple as that!

All right, Clyde is pitching for St. Louis and he's ready to go now. Harry is four for three today. He was on an island in the Pacific during the war for four years. I think it was Alcatraz. He's a big six-foot-four right-hander from Watch-It, South Carolina, who has a lot of stuff on the ball, although I see that right now the umpire is making him scrape it off. He has three children, and he's out there today, of course, with the usual number of fingers on his glove. Six. And now I see that the catcher is giving him the sign, which he always takes with his left eye. He has 20-47 vision, as most of you fans know, and he buys his socks at Abercrombie & Fitch. Last time he was up, two men died on base. The funeral is Friday at twelve o'clock.

Next . . . an open letter to Sandy Koufax. [*Struggles*

with envelope] Sorry, I can't seem to get the letter open. And now it's time to play ball!

SCHOOL FOR FIGHT ANNOUNCERS

"All right, class. Welcome to the school for prize-fight announcers. You men will go through a twelve-week course here, after which we'll get you jobs at out-of-the-way TV stations. Eventually you may work your way up to the big time. Riley, we'll start with you. Pretend we're on the air. Just make it up as you go along. Describe a fight for us."

"Okay. There's the bell for the first round and Clay lashes out with a right-hand punch that—"

"Wait a minute! What kind of talk is that? 'Lashes out?' Thank you, David Brinkley. What did you say Clay threw?"

"A right—hand—punch?"

"Not a right-hand punch. Just a *right*. Did it land?"

"No."

"All right. Clay misses with a right! Class! Repeat. Clay misses with a right."

"Clay—misses—with—a—right!"

"Okay, go on."

"Liston lands a left. Clay engages his arms to stop him punching in—"

"Hold it! Clay engages his arms?"

"Well, I meant that he—"

"I know what you meant. You meant he went into a *clinch*. So say Clay ties him up! Class."

"Clay ties him up."

"Fine. Continue."

"Both men are really fighting hard now. They're punching vigorously in the—"

"Cut! They're *not* fighting hard or punching vigorously."

"They're not? What *are* they doing?"

"They're throwing plenty of leather. Got it?"

"I think so. Both boys are throwing plenty of leather in the ring now—"

"Not in the ring! Never mind 'in the ring.' Just make it *in there. Both boys are throwing plenty of leather in there.* They're sparring around in there. They're mixing it up in there. It's all *in there.* Got it?"

"I see. Both boys are throwing plenty of leather in there and now there's a cut over Clay's right eye and the blood is falling on the—"

"Now, stop! What is that with the 'blood-is-falling' business? Blood isn't falling!"

"It isn't?"

"No. *The claret is beginning to flow.* Class!"

"*The claret is beginning to flow.*"

"O.K. The claret is beginning to flow . . . in there . . . and Clay is retreating a little—"

"He is *not!* He's *giving ground!* He's bicycling. He's back-pedaling. He is not retreating."

"Sorry. Clay is back-pedaling . . . *in there.* But he's very brave and it looks—"

"That's all! Boy, what an idiot! He's 'very brave.' Clay is *not* very brave!"

"All right. Clay is chicken in there—"

"Don't try to be funny! I meant you're supposed to say *dead game,* not 'very brave.'"

"All right. Clay is dead game . . . in there . . . where the claret is . . . and it's turning into an exciting match."

"No. Try pier-six brawl."

"Okay. It's turning into a real *pier-six brawl—*"

"Now you're getting the idea! Men, remember this rule. At no time are you to be original. If these lines were good enough for Graham MacNamee twenty-five years ago they're good enough for you today. Class dismissed."

AUTOGRAPH SEEKERS

The other day a fan told me his wife wouldn't let him into the house without my autograph. I have no idea how this cliché became so entrenched in our national vernacular since I assume that encounters with celebrities are, for the average citizen, rare. Yet practically every man who asks for an autograph claims that without it he will not be permitted access to his home and castle. I have a vision of thousands of men camping out in pup tents on front lawns all over America simply because I began to say no to requests for my autograph. It is to prevent this social cataclysm that I so readily accede to pleas for my signature.

Interviewers ask if the business of signing autographs is not a nuisance. Answer: it all depends. There are some entertainers who regard any request for a sample of their handwriting as an intolerable imposition, but I am not one of them. I know of one television master of ceremonies who, at a banquet in Washington, signed his autograph at the request of a middle-aged woman, and then when she said, "Will you make it out to my daughter,

Marilyn?" took the piece of paper back from her, tore it up, and turned away. There can be no excuse for such rudeness.

There are, of course, some autograph hounds we could do without. In case you'd like to make sure you don't impose on your favorite actor, here's a list of types that give autograph fans a bad name.

1. *Leaky-pen Louie.* This guy always hands you a 1927-model fountain pen, with the accent on the fountain. When you finish using his pen, you're streaked blue up to the elbow.

2. *Flash-bulb Phil.* This boy wants to take pictures, too. That's all right except he has a way of sneaking up and exploding his flash bulb about three inches from your face. This frightens you so badly you drop Louie's pen.

3. *Paperless Pete.* This worthy is really fantastic. He walks up to you with his hands in his pockets and says, "Gimme your autograph." When you reach for the pen and paper you presume he will produce he acts offended. "I ain't got a pen," he says. "Don't *you* carry one?" He borrows a pen and paper from somebody else in the crowd.

4. *Jeannie, the Jabber.* This girl is dangerous. She and her friends specialize in shoving sharp pens and pencils into your face as they fight for position. I lose more glasses that way.

5. *Bashful Ben.* This one is usually an adult. He acts as if asking for an autograph were the height of daring. "I wouldn't do this for myself," he says, looking at the sidewalk, "but my nephew . . ."

6. *Condescending Conrad.* A first cousin to Bashful Ben, this gentleman also wants the autograph for some-

one else. He explains his position in contemptuous terms. "We don't care much for your show at our house," he says bluntly, "but my sister's little boy . . ."

7. *Drygoods Dora.* This girl is not content with just a signature, she also asks for a tie or a handkerchief, and is hurt if you don't start to throw your haberdashery around.

8. *Bill, the Boss.* This fella believes you're his private secretary, the way he starts dictating. "Say, would you mind signing this one to Susabelle Klorbfelder on her seventeenth birthday with all good wishes and felicitations from her old friend Steve?"

Anyone for autographs?

ON SPECIAL TREATMENT

I imagine most people suppose that being a celebrity means one is afforded all sorts of special favors. For once most people are absolutely right. The reverse side of the coin, however, is completely overlooked. More often than not I find that having a familiar face involves me in confusion, inconvenience, and far poorer service than the average man would receive. Just the other day I shopped at a hardware and home-supply store for some plastic dishes. When I had located what I wanted I summoned a clerk. The conversation went something like this.

ME: Pardon me, I'd like to get some of this plastic dinnerware.

CLERK: Say, you look an awful lot like Steve Allen.

ME: Yes, I hear that all the time, I'd like to get some of these—

CLERK: You can't kid me. You *are* Steve Allen.

ME: [*Making no effort to kid him*] That's right.

CLERK: I thought so. Boy, we never miss you. Now, what was it you wanted?

ME: Well, it's the same thing I've been talking about. These plastic dishes. But I see only one box of them in that pink color. I'd like to get *two* boxes of the pink.

CLERK: Okay, Mr. Allen. Got 'em right here. Two boxes of pink dishes. There you are. Say, my wife'll get the biggest kick out of this. By the way [*Taking out a pen*], would you mind? My wife'll never let me into the house tonight if I come home without your autograph.

ME: My wife'll never let me into the house if I come home without these pink dishes.

At home I discovered (not really to my surprise) that *one* of the boxes of dishes was pink, the other blue. There's no villain in this story. The man behind the counter was a good-natured chap, and probably for all his other customers a very helpful salesclerk indeed. The point is that because my face is one that he sees regularly on television he concentrated more on me than on the business at hand. The incident is not isolated. I don't think I've gotten exactly what I ordered in a restaurant more than five times in the last year. There's almost always at least one mistake, and the more the waiter tells me how much he enjoys our program the more he gets the order all balled up.

In clothing stores I am given socks of the wrong size, shirts of the wrong color, and somebody else's underwear. In hotel lobbies I am given keys to other people's rooms, and at airports my baggage is sometimes put on planes going somewhere that I am not. All of these problems are, of course, vastly preferable to the proverbial poke in the eye with a sharp stick, but I mention them to indicate that being a public figure is not an unalloyed blessing.

THE REINDEER

In a relative world, humor is the most relative of things, so it would be difficult to say which of the thousands of interviews I have conducted was the most amusing. I can report, however, that one particular interview got the longest single laugh I ever heard on radio or TV.

Wandering up the theater aisle in New York one night I noticed three elderly women sitting together.

"Hello," I said. "Are you ladies in a group or alone?"

"Yes," said one of the ladies.

"Yes, *what?*" I asked.

"We are reindeer."

When something that definitely looks like a middle-aged woman identifies itself as a reindeer you can be reasonably certain that the ensuing conversation is going to be interesting. At moments like this I try to be extremely logical, for nothing will so clearly illumine eccentricity as displaying it against a background of rationality.

"You don't look like a reindeer to me," I said, "although stranger things have happened. My father was an Elk."

"That's right."

"I don't see how you could have known my father," I said, "but we're already digressing, although I'm not sure from what. Let me get to the point. What makes you think you are a reindeer?"

Martinis or manhattans?

Smith is attempting a conversion out there.

"We just *are*, that's all."

"All right," I said. "I didn't come down here to argue with you. But let me ask the lady on your right a question. What do you *do* in your capacity as reindeer, pull sleds for Santa Claus or something of the sort?"

"No," said the second woman. "We does all good thing."

"You does? I mean, you *do?*"

A light began to dawn.

"Tell me what one of the good things is," I said.

"We pay sick benefits."

"Ah, I think I understand. You are not really reindeer at all. You are human beings, just as I thought, but you belong to some sort of organization like the order of Moose or Woodmen of the World."

"That's right," the second lady beamed, not at all impatient at my denseness. "We belong to the Reindeer."

"Well, that's fine. Now tell me, what does the organization stand for?"

The three faces were blank.

"I mean," I said, "what do you do *besides* pay sick benefits?"

"Nothing, I guess."

"Have *you* ever received any sick benefits?"

"No."

"Have *any* of you ever received any sick benefits?"

At this there was a great flurry of whispered questions and craning of necks. It developed that scattered throughout the studio there were about twenty-seven other Reindeer, all of whom had come up on a chartered bus from a nearby city for a day in Manhattan. None of them, it appeared after a hasty check, had ever received so much as a penny of sick benefits.

"I don't wish to appear critical," I said, "but this seems to me to be a very unusual organization." Addressing the third woman, I said, "Exactly why did you become a member?"

The woman pointed a thumb at her companion. "Because she asked me to."

"And why did *you* become a member?"

The buck was passed again.

Incredibly, every woman in the room had become a Reindeer because some other woman had asked her to. None of them were able to offer the slightest information about the aims or purposes of the club. Desperately I returned to the matter of sick benefits.

"Perhaps," I suggested, "you're not really a social club at all. Perhaps you're more of an insurance company. But then again you all say that you have never received any of these benefits. That leads me to believe that either you are the healthiest group of women in the United States or that your treasury must be the most bulging in financial history, or both."

They all laughed good-naturedly.

"But still," I said, "I cannot conceive that not one cent has ever been paid out. And I don't see how you could all be in such perfect physical condition. There must be at least *one* member of your group who is laid up with something or other. I'd like to speak with the treasurer of your club. Where is she sitting?"

"She's not with us tonight," the lady on the aisle said.

"Oh? Where is she?" I asked.

"She's home sick."

The audience would not let me continue for almost two minutes.

FURTHER ENCROACHMENTS ON FREEDOM

As our society becomes more complex in structure and function, political philosophers give increasing attention to the limitations upon human freedom that accompany our technical evolution.

But there's one problem in this general area that, so far as I'm aware, is being overlooked and I unashamedly mount my soapbox today to rouse the rabble to a realization of their plight.

Let the John Birch Society worry about whether registration of firearms is a dastardly hindrance to the freedom of full-blooded American gunslingers. Let the members of Young Americans for Freedom concern themselves with the effrontery of a federal government that brazenly takes an interest in the economic freedom of *old* Americans down on their luck. Let the Ku Klux Klan ponder the new-fangled limitations upon the freedom of white racists to lynch, rape, and intimidate Negroes.

I shall, naturally, have more to say on these specific questions another day; at the moment I am concerned with not one of the more obvious encroachments upon freedom but the problem in one of its subtler aspects.

Consider, I pray, the matter of garbage.

The rules about garbage in many American communities have become increasingly strict in recent years.

I talked to our garbage man about this the other day

—after making an appointment, of course—and he gave me a new copy of the legal document that gives all the rules and regulations for putting garbage out and hauling it away.

This problem didn't exist when I was a child. We were quite poor in my neighborhood. We knew what to do with garbage—we ate it.

But nowadays the matter is considerably more complicated. In many American cities you can't just fill up garbage cans helter-skelter with any old thing, as you formerly could. You have to separate the slop. One container for tin cans. Another for leaves. Last week I didn't *have* any leaves. I had to go out and buy some, so the garbage man wouldn't get his feelings hurt.

Then you must have a separate can for bottles. And another garbage can for just paper. Out our way the actual garbage itself we have to gift-wrap.

If the trash-collection agencies become any more particular we'll eventually have to dehydrate our garbage and put it out in the form of small packets of a finely ground powder. Then at the close of the day, when he gets to the end of the line, the truck driver can simply add water and he'll have Instant Garbage.

Some people solve this problem by buying a garbage-disposal mechanism and putting it under their sink. These are effective devices, when they're working, but ours always seems to be breaking down. It's not disposing of much garbage, but it is disposing of a lot of my cash. In fact there's one plumber in our neighborhood who is putting his son through college with the money that he's earned repairing our disposal.

I'm calling an indignation convention at the city dump.
Citizens, to arms!

WHAT TO SAY WHEN IT RAINS

I have a new theory on the teaching of languages
based on the idea that the old theories are all wrong.
Usually when you're learning a new language you are
taught a lot of sentences like "I have a blue pencil" and
"Where is the hotel?" But I often go for weeks without
boasting about the color of my pencil or making inquiries
about lodging. On the other hand there are certain sentences that are unfailingly employed in response to
familiar stimuli; these are the phrases foreigners ought to
be taught.

For example, when it rains the following dozen sentences are rattled off, comprising a formal and unvarying
litany.

1. *The Simple Statement of Fact:* "Boy, look at it
   come down."
2. *The Lame Attempt at Humor:* "Nice weather for
   ducks."
3. *The Optimistic Approach:* "It'll stop. It's just a sun
   shower."
4. *The Pessimistic Approach:* "Boy, you'll never get
   a cab."
5. *The Scientific Approach:* "Let's see, does lightning
   come before thunder or is it the other way
   around?"
6. *The Antiscientific Approach:* "Those Chinese
   A-bomb tests cause all these storms."

7. *The Paranoid:* "Wouldn't you know it, I just washed the car."

8. *The Saintly Attitude:* "Well, the farmers sure needed this."

9. *The Resentment of Authority:* "That weatherman ought to have his head examined!"

10. *The Implication of Psychic Phenomena:* "It's funny, I *thought* of bringing an umbrella this morning."

11. *The Expression of Anxiety:* "I wonder if I left any windows open."

12. *Resignation to the Inevitable:* "I'm soaked to the skin."

Nothing, but I mean *nothing* else is ever said when it rains. It must have been murder on Noah and his group.

Of course, during the rainy season people sometimes *catch cold.* In that case there are only twelve things to say.

1. *The Interrogation:* "Whatsamatter, got a cold?"

2. *The Boast:* "Boy, I got a beaut."

3. *The Planting of Fear:* "Are you sure it's just a cold?"

4. *The Bubonic Plague Approach:* "Better not come near me."

5. *The Competitive Approach:* "You should have seen the one *I* had last week."

6. *The Scape-goat Theory:* "I never had a cold till they put in that damned air conditioner."

7. *The Thankful-for-Small-Blessings Approach:* "It seems to be settling in my head."

8. *The Attempt at Humor:* "If you take these new

wonder drugs you'll get over your cold in seven days. Otherwise you'll have it for a week."

9. *The Voodoo Wish:* "Ho-Chi-Minh should have this cold."

10. *The Travel-agent Pitch:* "What you need is a couple of weeks in Miami."

11. *The Cry of Doom:* "You sure it's just a cold? Friend of mine went last week just like *that*."

12. *The Appeal to Alcohol:* "One good shot of brandy'll knock it right out."

Mr. Berlitz, it's your move.

JOURNALISTIC CLICHÉS

When I was in Chicago recently I did a radio show one evening with Bill Ervin, the television critic, and we got to talking about—among other things—journalistic clichés, of which the greatest collector was that richly entertaining humorist Frank Sullivan. This reminded me of one particular sort of newspaper cliché, the perennial pictures, the shots that you see year after year. The faces and names change, but somehow the photographs themselves seem timeless.

Let me recall a few of them for you. First, there's the close-up of "The First Robin."

Then there's the standard "Ground-hog Day" shot. It figures that they get this one out of the old files because doing so seems more sensible than sending a photographer to wait around on somebody's damp lawn for hours to see if a particular ground hog emerges from a particular hole.

Number three on my list is "The Lost Child in the Police Station." The chief subject is a little boy or girl, anywhere from two to six years old, who has been lost in some public place, usually at a beach or a world's fair. The child is wearing one of the policeman's hats and is licking an ice-cream cone.

Then during almost any unusually hot spell you can usually count on seeing that old classic, the "Eggs Frying on the Sidewalk" (or on the top of a parked car).

The reverse of this shot is the picture taken during the winter months when members of "The Polar Bear Club" —masochists who seem to enjoy swimming in icy cold water—go out to the nearest lake, river, or ocean and splash about happily amidst the ice and snow.

Another classic is the picture that shows where a luckless motorist drove his car over an embankment or off a bridge. Not only do you observe the car lying at the bottom—usually overturned—but you see a dotted white line showing the path that it took through the air.

Then there are two standard shots that come under the heading of travel. In one you see a motion picture actress or starlet, mink coat and mouth both held wide open, standing on the steps of an airplane; in the other you see another motion picture actress—or perhaps even the same one—always with legs crossed, sitting on the rail of an ocean liner as her ship enters or leaves the local harbor.

If you can think of any other old standards, drop me a note about them and I'll share your observation with the rest of our readers.

OVER THE WAVES

Wavers seem to have been spawned by television. I say seem, for the waver has actually been with us for many years. I'm sure you remember seeing him in the newsreels. Sometimes his gesticulating was more or less in keeping with the mood of the event; after all, it isn't surprising to see men waving at baseball games or prize fights. But often the waver has pursued his annoying custom at occasions of great disaster. The scene: a train wreck. A long shot of railroad cars strewn in dizzy formation along a roadbed. Medium shot of one of the cars as rescue workers bend to their grim task. In the foreground, in shocking contrast to the air of tragedy that prevails, we see a couple of smiling goofs waving at the camera.

The wavers of television are, of course, usually just having a good time in more jovial surroundings, but there have been occasions when the mood of romantic musical numbers has been completely destroyed by the sight of a frantic hand waggling back and forth in an audience. A few years ago our *Tonight* show was honored one evening when Sid Caesar and his crew presented a satire of our program that involved Carl Reiner as "Alan Stevens" and Sid as a contestant doing a routine in the audience. Sid performed the sketch in the middle of his own audience and I found it hilariously funny—for the first few minutes. After that the real visitors sitting in front of Sid suddenly realized they were on camera and began waving and making faces. They proved such a distraction that neither the studio audience nor the viewers at home could concentrate on the professionals' performance.

Wavers break down into several categories. First there's the Rib-Poker. As soon as he sees himself on the studio TV monitors he jabs an elbow into the rib of his companion, points, and says, "Look, we're on."

Then there's the Narcissist, who is so infatuated with the sight of his own face on the screen that he becomes completely oblivious to everything else. He does not hear the interviewer's questions, he is no longer interested in the program, and he shows a blithe disregard for those seated nearby. He just sits and smiles and waves, at himself of all things. He can be deadly because often his waving is done while you are trying to interview the person sitting behind him.

Another type we will always have with us is the Sneak. He seems to realize that he really shouldn't be waving, so he does it with a surreptitious air, looking in one direction and waving a seemingly disembodied hand in the other.

Lastly there is the Boy Scout, so called because he works both arms wildly, as if he were sending flag signals to a distant mountaintop. He has been known to knock off the hats and muss the hair of women in front of him. I hereby nominate as the Eleventh Commandment, "In a television audience thou shalt use thy hands for naught save applause."

TIMES MAN CLASHES WITH SPOUSE

"Morning," said the headline composer's wife as she set the small glass of orange juice on the Formica-topped table. "How did you sleep?"

"Husband Passes Sleepless Night," said the man. "Blames Mate."

"Now don't hand me that," the woman said. "How do you figure it's my fault? What did I do?"

"Wife Talks in Sleep," said the man. "Hint Crisis."

"All right," the woman said. "Out with it. What's on your mind? What are you building up to?"

"Long Island Couple Mull Vacation Plans," said the man.

"What good would that do?" the woman demanded.

"Mountain Air Cure for Sleep Talk Claims Noted Medic."

"Noted, my eye," the woman said. "Doc Schiller knows you want to go to Lake Takawanda again this year and he's just telling you what you want to hear."

Angrily the man buttered a piece of toast.

"Hint End to Parley," he said in a surly tone. "Principals in Vacation Talks Report No Progress."

The woman silently put two pieces of bread in the toaster. She then measured out a spoonful of instant coffee and put it into the man's cup. He looked up hopefully.

"Spouse in Reconciliation Bid," he said.

"The hell," she snapped back. "I'm just trying to put an end to this whole silly conversation. Why don't you talk like a human being, anyway?"

The headline writer chomped disconsolately on a crust of bread.

"I've promised mother we'd spend at least a week with her this spring," said the woman. "And after all, Westport is on the water. Thousands of people vacation there."

"Plan Vacation for Mind, Not Just Body, Advises Medico."

"Medico-schmedico," snapped the woman. "You keep putting your own ideas into Doc Schiller's mouth!"

"Contact with In-laws Common Cause of Nervous Tension."

"Says who?"

"Many Scientific Truths Long Known by Ancients."

Her mouth a thin line, the woman sat staring into her coffee.

"Hope Seen," her husband said unexpectedly, "in Vacation Talks."

"I'm listening."

"Why-don't-you-leave-a-week-early-and-visit-with-your-mother-at-Westport-and-then-when-I-get-off-on-the-seventeenth-the-two-of-us-will-head-for-our-little-cabin-in-the-hills-and-get-in-lots-of-fishing-and-it'll-be-almost-like-a-second-honeymoon-whadda-ya-say?"

The woman rose, walked around to the man's side of the table, and sat on his lap.

"Compromise Proposal Accepted," she said. "Parley Concludes on High Note."

They kissed.

DANGER IN THE OFFICE BUILDING

I had barely left my own office and turned down the hall toward the water cooler when I saw him. He was closing in fast, walking head down, a sheaf of papers in his hand.

For a split second I froze. Then, moving backward in three quick steps, I slipped into the office and closed the door. Back pressed to the wall, I heard him hurry past.

Deciding against a drink of water I returned to my desk and had my secretary order a carton of cold orange juice from the drugstore downstairs. After all, I had already passed Harbach in the corridors three times that morning. A fourth encounter would have been beyond both of us.

I mean, what are you supposed to say to people you keep passing in the halls all day?

If you work in your own shop or drive a truck you probably meet the same people every day all right, but you meet them only once. You say, "Hiya, Mabel," or "How are you, Gus?" and that's the end of it. But if you work in a large office building things are different.

Oh, it doesn't look like much of a problem in the morning when you first come into the building. You meet a fellow as you get on the elevator and you say, "Morning, George," and he returns the salutation and that's that. This first meeting is only a primary barrier in the obstacle course that your day has, in the instant, become. It's a low hurdle, easily cleared. But sometime within the next hour or so—since people who work in office buildings rarely stay at their desks very long but are given to a great deal of walking purposefully down corridors—it is inevitable that you will meet George again.

It will be fortunate in that event if one of you is doing something besides just walking. For example, if you are bending over to tie a shoelace or George is getting a drink of water there is at once established a subject for conversation.

"Drinking some water, eh, George?" you can say.

"Keeping those shoelaces tied, eh, pal?" he can respond.

But if neither of you is doing anything except *walking* the problem begins to assume definite proportions.

Obviously you can't say "Walking down the hall, eh, George?" I don't know quite what you *can* say, you understand; I only know you can't say *that*.

Careful observation establishes that this second encounter almost invariably differs little from the first, except that the "Good morning's" are now changed to "Hi's," and the cheerful tone that characterized the matinal greeting has given way to a certain wary lack of expression.

With the third meeting you have come fully to grips with the situation and now have but two alternatives. You can either exchange a mutual chuckle or *one* of you can chuckle while the *other* says "Getting to be a habit."

A report has come in from the field that a jaunty soul did once attempt "Say, are you following me?" but it is not recorded that his lame effort at relieving tension was successful.

The fourth encounter is somehow the worst. You can laugh at the third and marvel at the fifth, but the fourth will certainly defeat you unless you enjoy a stroke of luck. As George approaches you eye each other desperately, minds racing. If fortune smiles, George might have papers in his hand. This entitles you to try even something as inept as "Working overtime, eh?" but since George is your only audience and you have relieved him of the responsibility of filling the breach his gratitude will render his critical powers inoperative and he will probably respond gratefully, "You know me," or perhaps even, "Yes, *sir!*"

The fifth time it is *de rigueur* to chuckle again. Keep

the order in mind. Chuckles are apropos the third and fifth time around. The sixth time one must be on guard against a surly note that is wont to introduce itself. Antagonism can be felt in the electric air. You nod and George winks. The seventh time you wink and George nods. There has never, to my knowledge, been an eighth time. You have exhausted your creative capacities and it is obvious that you cannot pass George and pretend not to see him.

So you stay at your desk, if you are smart, or venture from it only after careful scouting of the terrain. If passage or egress is vital, approach closed doors warily and beware of corners.

Good luck.

SPEECHES AND LETTERS

"Good evening, ladies and gentlemen, and in conclusion . . ."

(from a speech by Steve Allen)

If Allen the writer, as seen in the previous chapters, differs substantially in style and effect from Allen the television comedian, there is an even more readily perceptible difference in Allen the speechmaker.

Most of his speeches are made before audiences that differ greatly from those who attend his television programs. In the first place, instead of being admitted free they have probably paid a substantial amount for access to the dinner, luncheon, or banquet. Secondly, instead of a cross section of the American people, they represent more often than not a special interest group, all members of the same profession or organization, or all friends of the same guest of honor.

Given these circumstances, certain vibrations are stirred in Allen that set loose an uncanny empathy. Through a combination of advance checking on appropriate details and instinctive feeling for the requirements of the occasion, he can become a medicine-oriented comedian among doctors, a movie-wise laughmaker among film men, a returning home boy among Arizonans or Chicagoans.

In Allen's light yet pointed banter before such audiences one can detect qualities not unlike those of the late Robert Benchley. It is not so much that Benchley's wit influenced Allen (though Steve's admiration for the style has often been openly expressed), but rather that his personality, especially in situations like these, tends naturally in the same direction.

Most of Allen's speeches, after starting out on an improvised, humorous level to relax the audience, later proceed to a serious discussion of the particular subject that concerns his listeners. In several of the examples that follow, the humorous passages (or what is recalled of them) have been excerpted and the rest excluded.

REMARKS AT THE SCIENTIFIC SEMINAR
CONDUCTED BY THE MEMORIAL HOSPITAL
OF SOUTHERN CALIFORNIA,
SUNDAY, JANUARY 26, 1964

Good evening, ladies and gentlemen.

I am extremely honored to have been invited to address this distinguished assemblage this evening, although I am sure the question might have occurred to you, Why should a television entertainer be speaking at a medical convention?

The answer is that I happen to be a member of the profession that has brought you *Medic, Dr. Ben Casey, Dr. Zorba, Dr. Kildare, The Nurses,* and *The Eleventh Hour*—not to mention the countless programs that *need* a doctor.

But this is not the only reason why I'm glad to be present. It so happens that my oldest son, Steve, Jr., is attending the University of California at Berkeley, where he is taking a premedical course. Judging by his progress so far I believe he will probably end up in premedicine, but that's another story.

Needless to say, I am gratified to be in the presence this evening of so many distinguished representatives of the medical profession, one of whom has just introduced me—Dr. Ray La Scola. Dr. La Scola, as some of you may be aware, is the man who has succeeded in growing hair by hypnosis.

Unfortunately it did not grow on his *head*.

Most of it appeared, as I recall, on the palms of his hands.

But at least the achievement represented a great breakthrough and, as you medical men know, every great advance has modest beginnings.

As I was thinking over, during dinner, what I might say when I spoke to you, I happened to glance through the pamphlet that outlines the program for this seminar. It has been my observation that at seminars and conventions of this general sort there are those dedicated workers who devote a great deal of time and energy to the creation of these pamphlets and brochures, but all too often the membership and their wives do not pay sufficient attention to these brochures.

So for those of you who might have overlooked the folder which is on your table at this moment I am going to briefly leaf through it and draw your attention to certain highpoints of the proceedings of the last few days.

Things got off to a flying start Monday morning, January 25, at 9:30 with an address by Dr. Daniel Lang on the subject "Recent Developments in the Treatment of Shock Due to Hospitalization Bills."*

Then at ten o'clock Dr. Sydney Finegold discussed "The Problems of Baldness in Women, and How to Tell Bald Women from Bald Men."

Saturday afternoon at 1:30 Dr. Alfred Knudsen spoke on "Recent Advances in the Field of Recent Advances."

And at two o'clock, you will recall, there was a pair of stimulating speeches: "Diagnosis and Management of Breakdown," by Dr. Ralph Wallerstein, and "Breakdown of Diagnosis and Management," by Dr. Arthur Samuels.

And at three o'clock Dr. Matthew Block gave a talk titled "Studies of Hypertension Resulting from Medicare," followed by an interesting address by Dr. Ernest Beutlar, who spoke on "The Dangerous Side Effects of Antihistamine" and "The Dangerous Side Effects of Pro-Histamine," which gave evidence of Dr. Beutlar's well-rounded grasp of the situation.

I'm sure none of you will forget the two fine talks that opened the proceedings Sunday morning: "A Discussion of Morganstern's Disease," by Dr. Wallerstein, and "A Discussion of Wallerstein's Disease," by Dr. Morganstern. These two men have worked up quite a program together and are available as a team, I understand.

Then at 9:30 there was a talk on "The Importance of Good Grooming," by Dr. Zorba, followed by a remarkable address by Dr. Clarence Berne, who used color motion pictures. Dr. Berne, as many of you are aware, is the

---

* This joke and those that follow are based on the actual titles of talks given. Sample titles were "Recent Advances in Antibiotic Therapy," "Recent Advances in the Management of Urologic Infections," "Diagnosis and Management of Anemia," "Recent Developments in the Treatment of Parkinson's Disease," etc.

man who recently exposed the facts behind a well-known television advertising campaign, for it was Dr. Berne who revealed to the public that the children who used Crest toothpaste had fewer *teeth*.

Next, at 10:30—as you will see by consulting your program—there was a coffee break, followed at 10:45 by an address by Dr. Wiley F. Barker titled "Psychological Implications of the Coffee Break."

Then at 11:15 we all enjoyed hearing Dr. Paul De Camp ask the question "Is It Perhaps Cancer That Causes Smoking?"

For my own part I thought that the highpoint of the seminar was reached this afternoon at 1:45 when we heard the excellent talk "Fear and Neurotic Behavior," by Arthur Clinco.

I also enjoyed the talk titled "Fear and Neurotic Behavior *in* Arthur Clinco."

I understand that canceled at the last minute from the program was an address titled "Fear and Neurotic Behavior *Induced by* Arthur Clinco."°

But, all seriousness aside . . .

From this point Allen's remarks were of a serious nature.

BOOK-AND-AUTHOR LUNCHEON REMARKS

The following fragments are from a largely ad-lib address made by Allen for a book-and-author luncheon in Philadelphia sometime during 1956.

° Dr. Clinco is a noted psychoanalyst and associate professor of psychiatry at the University of California at Los Angeles.

Gretchen Finletter spoke first today about the problems facing today's woman. She pointed out that the home-maker of our time must be a teacher, laundress, maid, hostess, nurse, glamor girl, cook, citizen, woman of mystery, etc., etc.

She also referred to man's attempt to answer the question "Who Am I?" in his search for his identity.

The next speaker was Cameron Hawley, author of *Executive Suite* and *Cash McCall.* He warned that readers must not attempt to "identify" the characters, places, and events in his books. They are, he said, simply creations of his own imagination. By way of example he referred to the Hotel Ivanhoe, which figures importantly in *Cash McCall.*

"You must not think," he said, "that this is an actual hotel, although the story does take place in the city of Philadelphia."

The following are, to the best of Allen's recollection, his remarks:

* * *

It's wonderful to be here in [*Business of checking name of town on piece of paper taken from breast pocket*] . . . er . . . Philadelphia. It's not that I don't know where I am, it's just that I make so many of these appearances I . . . well, sometimes I *don't* know where I am. Often, of course, it's just due to my own carelessness in not carefully reading the letter of invitation that people send me.

Just last week, for example, I accepted an invitation to address a group of people I thought were connected with Simon & Schuster. I found out I had agreed to speak at Simon's Shoe Store.

Incidentally, this is not my first visit to your fair city. I appeared here about two years ago in a play named *Pink Elephant*. Possibly some of you may recall it. I hope not.

Be that as it may, however, it is good to be here this afternoon and to hear such fine addresses as those rendered by Miss Finletter and Mr. Hawley. I'm not sure what else Miss Finletter's address was, but it seemed to me to be the greatest argument for polygamy that I had ever heard. I was intrigued, too, by her reference to a philosophical point that seems to be particularly popular with our contemporary writers and thinkers. Namely, the matter of man's inquiry into his identity, as represented by the question "Who Am I?"

If I may say so, I think our writers are harping on this theme too much. I know they got me worried about the matter, so I looked into it and I found out what I am and I don't like it and I wish they had minded their own business. I was much happier before.

I also was fascinated by Mr. Hawley's remarks about his sources of inspiration. Possibly because my own stories are often related to reality one thing that has impressed me about Mr. Hawley's work is the great illusion of reality that it conveys.

To give you an idea of what I mean, I called down from New York this morning to the room clerk here at the Warwick and asked if I could reserve a room. He said, "I'm sorry, we're all filled up here but I *can* get you into the Ivanhoe."

Of course, books are interesting to me in almost any particular. I make it a practice to plug certain books on my TV program when the opportunity presents itself. I often say to my viewers, "You are watching too much TV.

You should read more books." You may wonder whether this sort of thing does any good. Well, I have ample proof that it does—my rating is dropping.

For another example, just the other night I held a book in front of one of our cameras and strongly urged people to lay hands on a copy at all costs. Within twenty minutes after I referred to this book it was stolen by one of our stagehands. Don't ever underestimate the power of TV.

I notice by a pamphlet that I find has been placed on all the tables here today that the theme of the luncheon is expressed in this quote from Chaucer: "On books for to read I me delight."

I believe Chaucer wrote this sentence when he was four years old. At least I hope so. There's another body of opinion that holds that Chaucer wrote this sentence when he was fully grown, but that the Chaucer involved was Sam Chaucer who ran a meat market in Forest Hills and never got beyond the third grade.

In any event, we should all read more books since I am sure none of us would ever want to be guilty of writing a sentence like "On books for to read I me delight."

SPEECH TO PHOENIX, ARIZONA, CHAMBER OF COMMERCE
APRIL 27, 1960

Since Allen had started his broadcasting career in Phoenix, Arizona, the city has ever since regarded him as a hometown product. In April of 1960 he was finally able to accept one of the many invitations to return that had been reaching him in Hollywood and New York for several years.

The then governor, Fannin, as well as many other local and regional dignitaries, was on hand to pay his respects. Allen was introduced and made substantially the following address, which it is possible to reproduce in great part because it was tape-recorded. As he started to speak, the public-address system in the hotel ballroom where the welcome-home luncheon was being staged began to break down. A loud and disconcerting hum was heard for several seconds.

✻   ✻   ✻

[*Looking up*] I think something is landing. Thank you very much, Ray, Governor Fannin, and other distinguished guests. Can you hear me all right in the back of the room? [*Silence*] I guess that answers that question. Thanks. Does anyone else hear the humming that I hear, or is it just me?

Voice: Right here.

Let's make sure we can hear it very *well* then. I don't want anybody to have any *trouble* hearing the humming while I'm speaking [*Hums*]. There we are [*Flash bulb goes off*]. I'll take a dozen eight-by-tens of that. Now, then.

Actually I came over here to Arizona to speak about the public-address systems of this community. I am going to present this hotel with an endowment and when I come back I want to see new equipment here.

I'll be back in twenty minutes.

We're a few minutes behind schedule so I'm not going to take too much of your time today. We got off to a late start and it's really my fault. I left a call at our hotel this morning for seven o'clock but it didn't do too much good because I didn't get to bed until about 7:30.

I know you will be pleased that I'm not going to make anything that can be formally described as a speech. For one thing, I didn't realize I was going to be called upon until about eight weeks ago. But I'll stand up here and talk for a long time regardless.

It occurs to me that I might, just in passing, make a brief word of apology for the sportiness of my attire. It was recommended this morning by one of the fellows in the Chamber that I wear a dark business suit, but I'll tell you, it's been such a long time since I've done any dark business that I didn't think it was too important.

It is a commonplace to stand up almost anywhere and tell what a great pleasure it is to be there, and I guess I've had great pleasure in a great many places in the last few years, but it *is* a particular pleasure to be in this particular city for this reason. Of course, it's always gratifying for a television entertainer to stand up in front of so many people who can't turn him off.

I have, naturally, a great many warm and sometimes amusing memories of this city and the people in it. And one thing I have had occasion to remember since leaving it is that it is always very important to keep in touch with the old hometown. Because I have lived in a number of communities, I have more hometowns than most people . . . and that might be my excuse for not having at all times kept as fully apprised of developments as should have been the case.

I'll tell you a little story that is absolutely true. It might sound like a luncheon joke, but is true.

When I eventually moved away from Phoenix I retained an emotional attachment to it, kept up my subscription to *Arizona Highways,* but did not otherwise keep apprised of the particulars of the town's progress. Because of this I became involved, one winter's day of 1952, in the most embarrassing conversation of my life.

I happened to be Christmas shopping in Macy's and suddenly, among the sea of faces that milled about me, I saw one that I recognized and associated, however vaguely, with Arizona. Since I was working on television at the time the man recognized me at once.

"Hi, Steve," he said. "I'm Nick Udall."

The name rang a very soft bell. I had known a great many Mormons in Arizona (Wendell Noble and Joe Dana, two of my old station KOY colleagues, were of this faith) and I was aware that Udall was a well-known Mormon name.

"What are you doing in New York?" I asked.

"I'm here for the big game," he said.

The game wasn't big enough for me to have heard about it.

"What game is that?" I said.

"Brigham Young is playing N.Y.U. tonight at the Garden."

Ah, I thought, a clue! Since I knew that Brigham Young University was in Provo, Utah, I assumed that my friend was now affiliated with the school, probably as a teacher, athletic coach, or something of the sort.

"Are you living up in Provo now, Nick?" I said.

"No," he said, with a slight smile. "I'm still down in Phoenix."

"What are you doing there now?" I said.

"Oh," he said, almost apologetically, "I'm the mayor."

Naturally I felt like a boob. In trying to extricate myself as gracefully as possible from the conversation my mind seized upon the hazy recollection that another chap I had known in Phoenix had been interested in politics. But I could not recall his name.

"Say," I said, "what ever happened to that fellow who used to announce at Station KTAR down the street from us—it seems to me that he—"

"Oh," he interrupted. "You mean Howard Pyle?"

"Yes," I said. "What ever happened to old Howard?"

"Oh," came the answer, "Howard's the governor now!"

I don't remember how I finally retreated, but I know it was in extreme embarrassment.

At that point I began to be afraid he was a friend of Harry Truman's. I *knew* what *he* was doing.

But as I say, ever since then I have realized how important it is to keep in touch with the folks back home.

Jack Williams, who also, as you know, has been mayor, was responsible for the credit or blame, as the case may be, of getting me started in radio and consequently on the road to television and I don't really know if Jack realized when he hired me that I was probably the dumbest eastern city dude that ever came out west and went to work in this community.

I had lived most of my life in Chicago, after having been born in New York City, and I don't think I had been working on KOY very long before I was assigned one afternoon, along with Joe Dana, to go out and describe a big parade. I hadn't even *seen* many parades in my time and I had never seen a rodeo parade.

As I recall this was annual rodeo day, so I was up on somebody's roof, I forget just where, along Central Avenue here. Somebody at the other end of the line described the start of the parade and then gradually the procession got down to my neighborhood. Up to that day I had never even ad-libbed so much as a *good morning* to members of my family. All conversation in my life had been cut and dried, as it is for most people. I was frightened by the very idea of having to ad-lib a single word on the rodeo so I had made a great many notes. I put them down on the ledge of the roof and they immediately blew away. It hadn't been very breezy that season, but right then a breeze came up.

At that moment my ad-libbing career began and much to my fright at this point the parade came along. I was doing a fair job of description, I suppose, and saying, "Well, here they come and don't they look wonderful in their uniforms and I wish you folks could be here, and I wish I wasn't."

I was, as I say, getting along, describing what was passing me. At that moment a Boy Scout band came along, marching past our position, and I was describing the look of it, the sound of it, and at that point—the parade stopped!

I don't know if you've ever tried to describe a Boy Scout band for ten minutes.

I think I finally got down to describing their shoelaces. They weren't playing—or anything—they were just standing there, sweating in the sun.

It was such a frightening experience that I have never forgotten it. But later that day I made an even bigger fool of myself. I reported out to the stadium here where they staged the rodeo itself—the big events—and I was put up on the judge's stand. I remember Hoot Gibson was standing next to me. I'm sure he wouldn't remember it.

Anyway, all of a sudden cowboys began riding around doing things I'd never seen before. Naturally I didn't know the proper terminology for anything, so that the first thing I described was a *steer-milking contest*. Something theretofore unknown to biological science.

We began to get a few phone calls. I think some of them were from *steers*, as a matter of fact.

But through the simple process of working here in Phoenix for about three years I finally picked up a little of the local color and local language. I had a very happy three years of my life in this fine city.

*   *   *

That completed the humorous portion of Allen's remarks. He then launched into a prepared address titled "Morality and Nuclear War." At its conclusion the audience gave him vigorous applause, but subsequent editorials in the city's decidedly conservative newspapers made it clear that such matters were rarely discussed in the city, which at that point was launching Barry Goldwater toward that distant target, the Republican presidential nomination.

REMARKS AT THE BOHEMIAN GROVE (1961)

The Bohemian Grove is a sprawling mountain camp deep in California redwood territory, where each year over a thousand of the most powerful men in our society gather for several days of old-fashioned masculine fun and relaxation. In 1961 Allen was invited to attend one of the annual encampments.

By day at the Grove politicians rub shoulders with publishers, generals, artists, musicians, and business tycoons. By night all hands gather around campfires to sing, tell smoking-room stories, drink, and (since it may be a long walk to the nearest plumbing facilities) make occasional trips to the nether side of a lordly redwood.

The political coloration of the Grove is basically conservative. During his visit Allen heard one of the late President Herbert Hoover's last public addresses. Barry Goldwater has also been a Grove visitor. But Democrats and liberals are often welcomed, and for the most part the talk is small, nonpolitical, and casual.

Following is a brief portion of the almost totally unprepared remarks made by Allen before several hundred men at one of the Grove's centers; the reproduction is based on a few notes he made at the time. Monte Rio, mentioned by Allen, is a place to which he had heard frequent humorous references made and where, to judge by the smirks that always greeted these references, one might enjoy the company of representatives of civilization's oldest profession.

*   *   *

Good evening, gentlemen.

Well, I certainly am happy to be here in the Bohemian Grave—er, *Grove*.

You've got yourselves a nice little grove here, and if the uric acid doesn't kill the trees, I think everything ought to work out just fine.

As a city dweller I've been impressed by the wildlife, too. I'm not talking about your personal habits but about the fact that I've seen deer up in the woods, and the other night I saw a rat scuttling through the underbrush.

And that's really something, too, because I understand that some of these rats have to wait about fifteen years to get in up here.

The most remarkable thing of all though (and I give you this not as a matter of personal opinion but simply in my capacity as a newcomer and observer and reporter) —the most remarkable thing about the Bohemian Grove is that every man up here seems to be an old son-of-a-bitch.

Nobody here says, "Hello, Bill, how are ya?" or "How've you been, Gus?" The common greeting is "Well, well, you old son-of-a-bitch!"

As a private citizen I find this especially impressive because the fifteen hundred men up here are for the most part exceedingly distinguished personages, many of them national leaders. Believe me, it's quite a shock the first time you see someone walk up to the governor of your state and hear him say, "Well, Governor, you old son-of-a-bitch!"

Which reminds me of the old story about the fellow on the speaker's platform at a political rally who heard a disturbance in the crowd and called out, "Who called the governor a son-of-a-bitch?" And a voice from the audience answered back, "Who called that son-of-a-bitch a governor?"

And speaking, too, as a former private in the army infantry I must say that it's a pretty heady experience to be able to walk up to a four-star general here and call him an old son-of-a-bitch.

But all in all I've had a wonderful time up here, though

I'm damned if I can figure out why. I know I never got into Monte Rio.

And while we're on that subject I want to make an observation. I've heard about five hundred dirty stories in the past twenty-four hours, and I've heard a lot of boasting about activity in Monte Rio, and I just must say that I never heard so much *talk* and saw so little *action* in my life.

But it's been wonderful meeting so many of you gentlemen and seeing you with your hair down—those of you that have any left. And I've been very favorably impressed by the way that men who back home are kings of their hill forget all about questions of prestige here and just pitch right in and do whatever chores are assigned to them.

For example, I don't know if you gentlemen noticed it or not, but one of the stagehands who just moved the Steinway for me was Mr. Henry Ford. Now that may not seem particularly noteworthy in a place like this, but yesterday when I drove in here the fellow who parked my Ford was Charlie Steinway.

REMARKS AT THE FRIAR'S CLUB DINNER FOR BILL HARBACH AND NICK VANOFF JANUARY 30, 1965

Tony Martin, master of ceremonies for the evening—which included comedy entertainment by Mel Brooks, Carl Reiner, Bill "Jose Jimenez" Dana, George Burns, and Corbett Monica—introduced Allen as "a man who had the good sense to buy Polaroid at twelve."

* * *

Thank you, Tony, and good evening, ladies and gentlemen.

Yes, as you've been told, I did buy Polaroid at twelve. Unfortunately I *sold* it when I was fourteen, like an idiot.

But I'm extremely happy to be here this evening to pay my respects to two such close friends. We worked together for so many years and I have benefited greatly by their support. In fact, I've often gotten credit for things that they were responsible for. It was Nick Vanoff, for example, who actually discovered Andy Williams and Carol Burnett.

He discovered them in the back seat of a parked car.

But these two men are successful today, and they deserve their success. You can always tell, of course, when people have that certain something. I am reminded of the day, almost fifteen years ago, when two young men came to me just bursting with good ideas. They had great energy, a lot of ability. I knew they were going places. I'm talking about Panama and Frank. What happened to Harbach and Vanoff after that meeting I have no idea.

But—seriously—it's wonderful to see these two fellows working together so effectively when they come from such different backgrounds. Think of it. These two young men, one of whom is from the wrong side of the tracks, the other of whom *owns* the tracks . . .

Now of course you all know that Bill's father is the great American songwriter Otto Harbach. But what some of you may not know is that Nick's father was the great *Macedonian* songwriter Otto Vanoff.

You all know the wonderful songs written by Bill's father, but let me tell you about Nick's father.

Bill's father wrote "The Indian Love Call."
Nick's father wrote "The Armenian Love Call."
Bill's father wrote "Smoke Gets in Your Eyes."
Nick's father wrote "Smoke Gets in Your Nose."
  And he wrote it first!
Bill's father wrote "You Do Something to Me."
Nick's father wrote "I'll Do Something to You."
Bill's father wrote "The Touch of Your Hand."
Nick's father wrote "Your Feet Are Like Ice."
Bill's father wrote "Rosemarie."
Nick's father wrote "Morey Amsterdam."

Jayne and I have known Bill since his early days as a young fledgling actor, when the two of them worked at M-G-M. In fact that was Bill's professional name in those days, Fledgling Young. He didn't want to make it on his father's reputation. But his story is inspiring. He came to Hollywood, ladies and gentlemen, without a penny in his pocket. But with fifty thousand dollars in his briefcase.

Now I know that's an old joke. But Bill is no spring chicken himself.

You know, when I met these fellows they had already done great things in the early days of television. In New York, Bill had produced the *Jean Martin Show*, *The Nick Kenny Show*, and the *Late Weather Report with Nancy Berg*. These were milestones, ladies and gentlemen.

And at this same time, in Hollywood, Nick was producing the *N.T.G. Bathing Beauty Parade*, *Peter Potter's Platter Parade*, and the *Roller Derby*. Remember that great program *You Asked for It?* Well, Nick was doing a horror show called "*It Asked for You.*"

But it's a wonderful tribute, not only to these two men, but to our American way of life, that a wealthy young man from Park Avenue could work side by side for all these years with a poor Macedonian *immigrant*. But Bill is very graceful about his wealth. And so is his lovely wife, Faye. I remember seeing her with their first child several years ago as they sat in the back seat of a limousine on Park Avenue. The little girl was just a year and a half old at the time. I said, "Can she walk?" and Faye said, "Thank God she'll never have to!"

Today Bill and Faye have *two* fine children, and, like their parents, they're not at all spoiled by being so rich. Last Christmas their oldest little girl walked up to Santa Claus and said, "What can I do for you?"

But—seriously—Faye and Bill live a very simple life. They don't keep servants. They *hire* a lot of them, but they don't keep them.

And once again I say "but seriously," and this time I mean it, when I express my pleasure at being here this evening to be part of this program that is meant to convey the admiration and deep affection all of us feel for Bill Harbach and Nick Vanoff.

ADDRESS AT CBS-TV CLINIC
WALDORF HOTEL, NEW YORK CITY
MAY 2, 1952

At the close of a two-day series of meetings and lectures offered by Columbia Broadcasting System to visiting radio station owners desirous of opening up television stations, the network presented a farewell banquet on the night of May 2, 1952. Gathered on the Starlight Roof of New York's Waldorf-Astoria Hotel, the visitors were treated to a program of entertainment featuring Perry Como, Mary Healy and Peter Lind Hayes, Jackie Gleason, Sam Levenson, Edgar Bergen, and, last, Steve Allen. He was introduced in a warm and flowery way by Ed Sullivan, master of ceremonies for the evening, who had introduced some of the other performers in a manner peculiar to some long-time observers of the show-business scene. Such people are often wont to pride themselves on the earliness with which they have recognized talent and predicted its ultimate popularity, and this particular evening Sullivan had waxed voluble over his now justified divinations that various of the entertainers on the bill with him were fated for stardom. So warmly did the milk of human kindness flow from Ed, indeed, that he called for a gesture of appreciation on the part of the audience for his good friend and production associate Marlo Lewis of the CBS-TV production department.

Lewis, he explained, had functioned as chairman of the entertainment committee for the affair and had done the job that Sullivan had known he would. It was a great thing, said Sullivan, that a man could count on the assistance of an able partner, and since this partnership was one between an Irishman and a Jew it was particularly heartwarming that it should be so long-lasting and so genuinely friendly. In this sort of atmosphere Mr. Allen was introduced and made substantially the following remarks:

* * *

Thank you very much, Ed. I have no "act," ladies and gentlemen, so I'm not going to do one. I'm not, strictly speaking, going to *entertain* you at all. I simply have a few announcements to make before the evening's activities come to an end. For one thing I know it's very late and you're probably all anxious to get out of here and get to a cheaper hotel.

There's no particular reason, by the way, why I'm closing the show. Well, there is one reason. It's that all the other people have already performed. I'm the only one left.

It was a great honor to be introduced in such a flattering way by Ed Sullivan, although I don't believe he claimed that he discovered me as he has discovered some of the others who appeared here tonight. I always enjoy hearing Ed introduce people in his inimitable way. It's sort of a vicarious thrill to realize that here is a man who was on the spot, so to speak, when great talents were born. But I feel a slightly different thrill these days at various banquets and benefits when I see Ed Sullivan on the platform. For I remember that many years ago, when I was learning to read, I picked up a copy of a local paper one day . . . the *Yonkers Shopping News,* I believe it was . . . and I read a column written by a young newspaperman. Right away I realized that this fellow *had something.* I knew that some day he would do big things. You all know who I'm talking about—Walter Winchell.

Seriously, Ed is a great guy. His remarks about Marlo Lewis this evening came right from the heart. All of us talk about the brotherhood of man, but here is a fellow who practices what he preaches, and who is a genuinely warmhearted human being. I was particularly pleased to hear him point out that his friendship with Marlo represents an Irish-Jewish partnership. Perhaps most of you didn't know that Mr. Sullivan is Jewish.

I don't know what you're laughing at . . . just because they frequently misspell Marlo Lewis's name. His first name is Marl. His last name is *O'Lewis*. But printers get careless, you know how it is.

Before I go any further I'd like to make the announcements I came up here to make, and to remind you that I really am not going to take much of your time. First of all, if you'll look on your tables there you'll find a little card. In case you can't read yours because of the dim lighting I'll just point out to you what it says. "Gratuities for the waiters have been taken care of by the chairman of the committee." So that's that.

You may, however, leave a small tip for the chairman of the committee.

I hope you enjoyed the food tonight. Some of it we paid for, and some of it was contributed. The rolls, I think, were contributed by the Wonder Bread bakeries. I know these people quite well, for they formerly sponsored one of my programs. I don't believe I'll ever be able to forget one of their most common advertising messages. "Wonder Bread Makes Your Child Grow Eight Ways." My oldest boy looks like an octopus, but he certainly enjoys that bread.

That just about concludes my remarks, but before I actually close I'd like to say a few words on behalf of Columbia to tell you how much we've enjoyed spending these past two or three days with you. I have a copy of the program here with me and looking at it certainly revives a great many pleasant memories of this wonderful convention. I don't believe any of us will forget Mr. Van Volken—Mr. Volkvannen—Mr. Van Volkenburg—Mr. Stanton's opening address.

Another wonderful session was that presided over by CBS-TV's vice-president in charge of sales, Fred Thrower. That's right. Fred Thrower. And he certainly does.

But there's one thing you've got to admit about Fred. He's a stickler for results. Up at the network when they want results they call Fred in, and he stickles.

He's a go-getter, though. He doesn't wait for the sponsors and the agencies to come to him. He goes out and digs up new business all the time. Right now he's very interested in landing a new Proctor and Gamble account. It's for a brand-new product, a shaving preparation called Reversex. Interesting stuff. Works on an entirely new principle. You rub it on your face, it makes the whiskers grow inside, and you *bite* them off.

But that's the sort of thing that Fred gets behind. He's also the man who promoted, before he came to CBS, an entirely new departure in sun-tan lotions. Something called Shinola.

Looking at the next page of your programs you'll be reminded of the wonderful address by CBS's vice-president in charge of programing, Hubbell Robinson.

I'm quoting Hub here for a moment. "Television has changed from a baby to a giant in the short space of three years. We at CBS feel very deeply our obligation to mold better programs." That will give you some idea of where all those moldy programs are coming from.

But Hub has done a fantastic job for the network these past two years. You're all familiar with the program *Arthur Godfrey and His Friends*. Well, Hub had nothing to do with that.

He has been working on a few projects involving Godfrey, though, and he recognizes the value of Arthur's name to the industry. Hub has plans to put a new show on in the fall titled *Friends of Arthur Godfrey's Friends,* and if it's as successful as we all know it will be he's prepared to follow it with *Arthur Godfrey and His Enemies.*

But this is the least of Hubbell Robinson's distinctions. He has brought *Our Miss Brooks* to CBS television, and already he's at work on a sequel, to be called *Son of Our Miss Brooks.*

And do you know *Studio One?* Robinson is the man who produced *Studio Two.* Fred Thrower sold the latter show, incidentally, to Adam Hats, and you will see it on your screens shortly under its new title, *Studio Six and Seven-eighths.*

One of the highlights of the convention, to my mind, was the talk by Art Jacobson, of station relations. Art started, as most of you know, back in Des Moines, Iowa, at a small station, and he soon had all of his relations working for him. He's been at it ever since, working out of New York, with WCBS, and he coined its old slogan, "Your Friendly Independent Station." Of course, in those days it was a lot more independent than it was friendly.

*   *   *

LETTERS

It is commonly supposed that all humorists write nothing but excruciatingly amusing letters. Although some purveyors of humorous prose do compose letters consistent in style with their material written for publication, others frequently do not bother to summon up the cosmic muse in correspondence. Allen dictates an enormous amount of mail, but rarely bothers to write funny letters about either serious or trivial matters. Most of the humorous letters he has written are now untraceable, but carbons of a few samples do persist in his files. Several of these are reproduced below.

A Larchmont, New York, viewer wrote to Steve:

"Marie Torre of the *Herald Tribune* calls you a nonconformist. What else makes your approach to the ridiculous so pleasant, refreshing and amusing?

"Being at least on the edge of the age where opinions and arteries harden I would have had the conviction that yours would be a program that would *not* conform to the 'God-Bless-You' ending. Your August 5 program cracked this belief. . . ."

Allen's response:

"I agree that I am something of a nonconformist, although no man is a nonconformist in every respect. One respect in which I am willing to go along with the mob is that relating to a belief in God. Since I assume He exists I see nothing unusual or improper in occasionally expressing to my audience the wish that God might bless them, although I am quite aware that His decisions to do so do not depend at all on my suggestion.

"In any event, thank you for your good wishes."

The letter was signed, "Gesundheit, Steve Allen."

New York, N.Y.
April 5, 1952

Dean Myers
Columbus Dispatch
Columbus, Ohio

Dear Mr. Myers:

A dear, little old lady who makes a hobby out of saving articles about me and sending them to my office on a regular basis has provided me with a copy of your column of March 27.

The dear little old lady works for a commercial clipping service.

I found the article she forwarded hugely amusing. This was partly because I am huge and easily amused and partly because you whip up a superior column. I sampled it and found it eminently satisfactory and noticeably milder, with no unpleasant aftertaste.

As I recall (and I recall pretty well with the article lying three inches to the left of my typewriter) you said some nice things about *Songs for Sale*. Your only complaint was that you couldn't hear very well because you were interviewing me by telephone while so, at the time, were six or seven other radio-television editors scattered around the country.

If you think you were having trouble, consider my position. Have you ever tried to talk to eight people at once? Have you ever tried to explain to sundry telephone operators that eight different connections are weak? Have you ever been lonely? Have you ever been blue? Have you ever loved someone . . . just as I love you?

Be that as it may, and I'm not sure it is, I was the

person in the most uncomfortable spot during that conference-call and as such am in no mood to squander sympathy on undeserving columnists with tin ears.

I couldn't hear *any* of you very well. There was one voice that came in loud and clear from time to time but I was rattled to finally learn that it was my secretary in the next room.

Besides, I am a very busy man. Having to hang around the office to make that call that afternoon meant missing the regular Tuesday meeting of the Aqua-Velva After-Shave Club.

I don't want you to think I'm ungrateful, Dean, but I wouldn't be keeping faith with the little old lady down at the clipping service if I didn't occasionally speak my mind to you gentlemen of the press.

Best Wishes,
Steve Allen

March
Twenty-seventh
1 9 6 2

Mr. and Mrs. Steve Lawrence
1175 York Avenue
New York, New York

Dear Eydie and Steve:

Just before leaving town I heard about your accident on the elevator. I certainly hope that there are no serious effects from it. Thank God, at least, that it wasn't worse.

If I'd known you were going to fall down the shaft I would have accepted your invitation to go to the Copa;

I need the publicity right now. As you know, I saw *I Can Get It for You Wholesale* that night. I'm sure you had more laughs falling down the elevator shaft.

But seriously, folks . . . I hope everything is fine and dandy for you both. See you soon.

Love,
Steve

18th July, 1958

Mr. Groucho Marx.

Dear Groucho:

I am writing this letter from London, which has impressed me so far as one magnificent straight line. I keep thinking of funny things here and, since no one else understands me, I thought I would unburden myself to you.

I have spent the last four days here with two of my sons, Brian and Steve, Jr., and it is doubly interesting to see this land through their eyes as well as my own. In fact, I can see it much better through their eyes due to my being somewhat near-sighted. In any event, when you have a child who refers to Madam Tussaud's Waxworks as "Madam Toupee's Wax House," as Brian did the other day, you shall not have lived in vain.

Almost everything here is strange and fascinating and I highly approve of all of it, although there are complications:

The word for water closet here is LOO. It made me feel a little embarrassed to ask about the Battle of Waterloo.

The money evaluation is very puzzling to an American, especially a stupid one. But I think I have it more or less straight now. There are sixteen ounces to a pound. One pound is worth twenty shillings. A shilling is worth seven ha'pennies and a slug. There are three wickets to a florin, two florins to a guinea, three guineas to a polack, eight half-crowns to a quid, four tentacles to a squid, and a tuppence is worth four Bobs and a Charlie.

There seems to be scarcely a house or public building in London that does not have historical significance. I've had so many places of interest pointed out to me the past few days that all the descriptive speeches seem conglomerated in my mind into one brief lecture that goes something like this:

"That building on your left is Worcestershire House. It was built in 1693 at the corner of Eaton Place and Drinkin' Place by the Earl of Brylcreem for his mistress, the Duke of Shirestershire. And right over here you'll see the Admiralty Bastion, which was formerly called Westminister Bowling Alley and is widely known as the place that Keats never heard of. Those holes and spots along the side there were made during the Boer War. The heavy building stones were shipped to Africa, badly scarred, and shipped back for insertion into the forward wall, by way of adding a bit of color. Just across the mall moat there you'll see the Hempstead Convents, fabled in song and story as the scene of the Coldstream Boarwrestling Tournaments. It was on that very bench that Jonathan Swift was arrested for vagrancy and thrown into the King's Reach, which is the place where the Thames flows under the powder room of Buckingham Palace. It's a pity we're just a few minutes late or you could see the Trooping of the Colored People past the statue of Abraham Lincoln, which was erected in 1309 to commemorate the signing of Colonel Tom Parker's first legal contract."

Believe me, that is not much of an exaggeration.

You can have a lot of laughs here just reading the telephone book. There are so many names like Wellesley-Claremont and Sir Wrigley Spearmint, and that sort of thing. You also notice that many English writers and other men of note use three initials before their surnames, for example: J.F.S. Haldane, I.A.R. Wylie, etc. I've been telling people I worked in New York for a chap named R.C.A. Sarnoff!

I am off in the morning to Paris. You may never hear from me again!

> Sincerely,
> Steve

November
Fifteenth
1 9 6 0

Mr. Groucho Marx
1083 Hillcrest Road
Beverly Hills, California

Dear Groucho:

I was very touched by your kind letter of November 10 about *Mark It and Strike It*. It was good of you to say that my writing gave you "quite a lift." As you will recall, this is the second lift I have given you in recent weeks; the earlier one being out of Bob Six's swimming pool.

Come to think of it, I also gave you a lift the night

you fell down in the balcony of that theater on Wilshire Blvd. I must say that knowing you has been one of the most uplifting experiences of my life.

I greatly enjoyed your autobiography, too, and am moderately depressed by the fact that it was a lot funnier than my own. For some reason or other, when I get to a typewriter what comes out is usually rather serious stuff. I know that I seem like a clown on the outside, but deep down in my heart I'm a very silly person.

Jayne sends her love. We hope to see you and Eden soon.

Fondly,
Steve

ALLEN DIXIT

Though his success has been vast and continuous in the many areas outlined in earlier chapters, perhaps the main factor that has built Steve Allen's public image as a humorous personality is his ability to come up with isolated quips under a variety of circumstances.

The degree of humor and subtlety in these remarks varies enormously. Allen says, "If critics observe that few if any of the witticisms quoted here are timeless I will enthusiastically agree. It has long seemed to me that one reason that audiences laugh so heartily over exchanges such as these is that in most situations I come up with the same sort of joke anyone might if he had a minute or two to work the problem over. Consequently the average listener feels, albeit subconsciously, that 'That's *my* type of humor,' and so there is a sense of personal identification with my audience interview jokes that might not be felt toward a superior line created by, say, Sid Caesar's writers."

For the same reasons, the humor of Steve Allen cannot be pinned down or categorized in the same manner in which one can analyze and pigeonhole the work of a Jack Benny, Bob Hope, or a Jerry Lewis. Nevertheless, in the area of his ability to toss off verbal gags it is possible to subdivide these into a series of approaches, or subject matter.

For example, one of Allen's most typical verbal ploys is his ability to take literally a remark that was meant only figuratively, and thus to twist it to absurd effect. Following are some examples of the Allen brand of literal humor:

Author Richard Gehman recalls the occasion when he was interviewing Allen at the Absinthe House in New York. A stranger suddenly detached himself from the bar and ambled over, uninvited, to their table.

"I'll bet you don't remember me, Mr. Allen," he said.

"Gosh," Steve responded, apologetically. "I'm afraid I don't."

"Aw, come on," the stranger said, "don't hand me that. My name is Jack Clouse. Doesn't that ring a bell?"

"Ah, yes," Allen said. "Jack Clouse, the Bell-Ringer!"

Once when a friend said, "I see there's been another wildcat strike in Chicago," Steve replied, "Why don't they give those wildcats the raw meat they're striking for and put an end to it?"

When one of his four children asked him if he knew much about the Lincoln-Douglas debates, he said, "Yes. They were a series of debates between Lincoln Douglas and Seymour Pitkin."

Speaking of a political group that Allen considered inept, he said, "I was invited to sit on the committee, and if there's anything I'd like to do to that committee it's sit on it."

Many of Allen's ripostes have been based on extensions of well-known figures of speech, usually carrying the idea *ad absurdum.*

Paraphrasing a familiar speech from a well-known TV show, Allen once said, "The qualities of a good physician are these: the heart of a lion, the eye of an eagle, the hand of a woman, the yolk of an egg, two cups of flour, and three tablespoonsful of brown sugar."

Jayne Meadows Allen's father, the Reverend Francis Cotter, once said to Steve, "Our home had a fireplace so large you could walk right into it."

"I tried that once," Allen said, "and got the heck burned out of me."

Some of Allen's humor, instead of relying on manipulation of the vagaries of the English language, plunges into a world of sheer fantasy.

An item found in a notebook of Steve's:

"A man I knew had the habit of slapping himself on the forehead whenever he remembered he had forgotten something. He never did improve his memory but eventually he developed a receding forehead."

A father-son exchange:

BILLY: Daddy, will you get me my bathrobe?

STEVE: I'm on the phone right now. Get it yourself.

BILLY: I can't. It's up on a hook and I can't reach it.

STEVE: Then go stand in the corner and grow.

One night after moving to NBC Allen was being interviewed by all-night disc jockey Stan Shaw on WINS. Stan said, "Steve, we're all happy about the way things are going for you today, but what ever happened to CBS? Gosh, when they first brought you east you were going like a house afire. What happened?"

"The house burned down," Steve said.

Jim Collins, of the Willoughby, Ohio, *News-Herald,* tells the following story.

"If you watched Steve Allen's television show last

night, you may have seen your favorite *News-Herald* carrier on your living-room screen."

Allen mentioned that twenty-five carriers had won a trip to New York and were guests at his broadcast. During the audience warm-up period funny man Allen got off one of his best quips of the evening. He was calling for questions from the audience, and one of the carriers asked, "Did you deliver the *News-Herald* when you were a boy?"

"No," said Steve, "that was during the Depression years. When I was a boy I *stole* the *News-Herald*."

Under the heading of child psychology Steve tells the following story, of questionable authenticity:

My little boy used to have a problem about sucking his thumb and wetting his bed. I tried giving him positive and helpful suggestions as a means of dealing with the problem. After a few weeks of constant indoctrination and suggestion the result was remarkable. He stopped sucking his thumb.

Now he *wets* his thumb.

And sucks his bed.

At the League of California Cities luncheon on October 13, 1965, toastmaster Pat Buttram related the story of how, in the days when Sam Yorty was running for mayor of Los Angeles and was considered an unlikely winner, Yorty appeared on Buttram's program along with strip-tease artist Brandy Long. Pat commented that this appearance attracted so much attention that it may have had something to do with Yorty's being elected.

During Allen's remarks on this occasion he observed

that there was more to the story than Buttram had revealed and that the incident did indeed prove the
power of radio-TV in the political arena.

"Although it is not generally known," he said, "as a result of her appearance on the program that night Brandy
Long herself received over 200,000 write-in votes."

On another occasion the child of a friend strolled into
a room where Allen was waiting to see his parents and
announced that he had just done number one and number two. Steve told him to go try number three.

Allen, who keeps himself in good physical shape, observed recently:

"Everybody is working out these days, building up his
muscles. My wife goes to Elizabeth Arden's to work out.
And I happen to know that Elizabeth Arden herself works
out at Vic Tanney's."

Allen once wrote, "Almost all blunt humor pertaining
to sex leaves me cold, although I think those who say that
it is altogether improper per se to deal humorously with
this subject matter are wrong. Much, of course, depends
upon the circumstances in which the humor is created
and/or dispensed. A story suitable for telling in an army
barracks is clearly not often designed for delivery over
television—although a few comedians seem to have a
hazy understanding of such distinctions.

"I have the theory that those who spend the most time
telling stories of a sexual nature are usually those who,
to use the phrase of the streets, aren't getting any. Or
much. This observation has been borne out by the few
individuals with whom I have tested it. And someday I
may write a piece about women who employ foul lan-

guage and tell off-color stories in mixed company. Off-hand I can think of few things more disgusting than hearing a scatological story or a vulgar oath from a beautiful woman. It is a small tragedy that more women in our society are not aware that many men share this opinion, and it is doubly a pity for the girls involved since some of them use gutter language because they think it puts men at ease or even has a certain stimulating effect. The use of a plain Anglo-Saxon dictionary language between lovers is one thing, but foul and supposedly comic talk between casual acquaintances of opposite sex is a universe away."

Allen's reservations about the use of sexual comedy do not extend to the dangers inherent in the use of macabre or sadistic humor. Perhaps because of his basic good taste and good nature he has frequently been able to get away with cracks that fall into this category without causing any offense to the vast majority of his audience.

"Freud pointed out," says Allen, "that there is a sadistical emotional background for a great deal of humor. The reasons are somewhat mysterious. One theory is that laughter itself may have originated in the victory, the cry of glee, the expression that seems to say 'Ha, ha, I've got you down, you son of a gun!' but obviously the cave man or vindictive approach to humor is only one very small aspect of it and doesn't explain the over-all reason for laughter. Once more, I don't think it is truly sadistic. We laugh when we see someone trip on a banana peel; but if we find he has really hurt himself seriously our laughter fades pretty fast."

Speaking of sick humor in general, Allen once observed that these jokes appeal only to the young, the comparatively sophisticated, the hip, and the educated; they may therefore be an expression of nonconformity.

It is possible that the very man who would create or relate a joke about Harold Russell's prosthetic appliances would be extremely and sincerely sympathetic were he to come in contact with Russell personally. Conversely, there are people who would be very critical about the joke but who, if they were brought into Russell's company, would not give him the time of day. So there is no necessary relationship between sadistic tendencies and sick jokes.

Describing the welcome given him when he returned to Phoenix, Arizona, one of his hometowns, Allen said, "It was a big homecoming celebration. A band of seventy-five musicians met our train at the station. The train ran right over them. It was horrible."

Leonard Traube, of *Variety*, recalls the night that a guest asked Allen what choice he would make if his doctor told him to choose between cancer and cigarettes.

"I'd give up cancer," was the response.

When told that Dr. John Bodkin Adams, the English physician suspected of murdering at least one of his elderly female patients, had been acquitted, Allen said, "He may be innocent, but I bet it'll be kind of quiet around his waiting room the next few months."

When told that the nation that has the highest suicide rate is Sweden, the American city with most suicides is San Francisco, and the profession most prone to suicide is that of bartender, Allen remarked, "I know a Swedish bartender in San Francisco who is plenty worried."

Allen can also add a ghoulish twist to a conversational

cliché, as for instance in: "That man needs a prefrontal lobotomy like he needs a hole in the head."

Steve did a line on the show once about a hearing aid. His wife Jayne asked him, "Did any deaf people register complaints about the joke?"

"Yes," Steve said, "one woman complained."

"Did you have an answer for her?" Jayne said.

"Yes," said Steve, "but she couldn't hear it."

Gardner McKay, of *Adventures in Paradise*, was telling Steve about his travels through the Near East. "A Bedouin," he said, "is very superstitious. In fact he will see his wife die before he will call in a doctor."

"So will my uncle," observed Allen.

A friend said that a not very attractive couple were expecting.

"Good," Allen said. "I hope it's a child."

The heavy southern California rains of 1962 destroyed part of his hillside property in Encino. Shortly thereafter he told his TV audience, "I just bought some very expensive real estate out in the Valley. It's a beautiful four-and-a-half-acre landslide."

Such sensitive and often controversial subjects as race, religion, and politics, though they play a minimal role in the basic quality of Allen's humor, have occasionally triggered his written or verbal thrusts.

Once, upon receiving a publisher's list of new books, he wrote back as follows:

"I was amused by one particular listing on page forty-one: *The Tall Book of Bible Stories*. Has anyone ever ordered this under the title *The Book of Tall Bible Stories?*"

Publicist Marvin Cohn once told Allen that Pope John

XXIII had recommended that boxing be abolished because Jesus Christ was not a fighting man.

"He's forgetting one thing that Christ had," Allen said.

"What's that?" Cohn asked.

"Right cross," was Allen's answer.

Hearing about the success of actress Irish McCalla on a TV adventure series, Steve claimed to have discovered a new jungle huntress named Jewish Magilla.

A Los Angeles citizen, defending some members of the John Birch Society, said, "It's not fair to blame these people for all the foolish things that Robert Welch has said and done. Why, some of these people are the backbone of society."

"If they are," Allen responded, "then this nation needs a good chiropractor."

From time to time, of course, Allen has displayed his talents as a mordant and articulate social commentator. His remarks, though they often make a valid political point, are usually laced with a delicate humor. He once wrote:

"Much political mischief and nonsense is traceable not to malice but to a clumsy use of labels. And even when labels are used correctly they tell very little about a man. A socialist, for example, is not *only* a socialist. He may also be a violinist, a Unitarian, a chess player, a husband, and a comforter of the afflicted. And when you kill the socialist you also kill the violinist, the Unitarian, the chess player, the husband, the father, and the Good Samaritan."

These observations were made in a 1963 article for the ultraconservative *National Review* and entitled "How to

Attack a Liberal." The article also included a typical touch of Allen satire:

"Audubon Society members interested in the *Golden-Throated Warbler*, the *Red-Breasted Robin*, and the *Great Horned Owl* must detect a familiar ring in those hardy denizens of the political forest, the *Black-Hearted Communist*, the *Die-Hard Reactionary*, the *Moss-Backed Conservative*, and the *Fuzzy-Minded Liberal*. In any event, the hunting season appears more open than ever and arrows fly in all directions."

Though he has remained firmly nonpartisan in his choice of political guests on TV through the years, Steve's liberal Democratic inclination has always been plainly in evidence. In this he is one of a large majority of show-business figures; there are practically no conservative entertainers of consequence, and few conservative actors.

On the night of January 7, 1963, Steve was a participant in a memorable show held at the Memorial Auditorium in Sacramento, California, to celebrate Governor Pat Brown's victory over Richard M. Nixon. The star-studded extravaganza included Frank Sinatra, Dean Martin, Joey Bishop, Jo Stafford, Jimmy Durante, Eddie Jackson, and Dorothy Dandridge.

As more than four thousand of California's members of the Democratic party adherents listened, Steve addressed them:

"I think we should be particularly happy that a Democratic candidate was victorious, because if Richard Nixon had won, you'd be sitting here listening to Raymond Massey and Ronald Reagan."

During a warm-up before his broadcast one evening a

woman introduced herself to Steve, then said, "I'm from Arkansas, and I've lost some of my friends."

"You mean," said Steve, "because of the Faubus incident?"

Occasionally a sensitive issue such as race or politics can bring out a rather biting edge in Steve Allen's humor.

During a studio warm-up, Steve went down into what he calls the "snake pit" and began answering questions. One lady asked, "Mr. Allen, what is Gene Rayburn's nationality?" Announcer Rayburn himself volunteered that he was Croatian.

"Is that so?" Allen said to Rayburn. "Well, you learn something new every night." Then Steve turned to the audience and said, "Any more impersonal questions?"

The pun, which can be the highest or lowest form of humor according to the skill or clumsiness with which it is employed, has frequently entered into Allen's spontaneous dialogues, as well as his writings. Asked to translate that Latin sentence dear to the hearts of all freshmen, *Omnia Gallia divisa est in tres partes*, Steve freely interpreted it as "Some people have enough gall to start a Third Party."

In Allen's book *The Funny Men* he tells how the world came to be divided into the various time bands, or zones. The man who devised the plan was a nineteenth-century Norwegian scientist named Andersrag. Alex Andersrag. To this day you will hear people talk about the Alex Andersrag Time Band.

Allen's wife is by now long accustomed to playing an unwitting straight woman. She never knows whether she's going to get a serious answer or something like this.

JAYNE: What are the inhabitants of Ghana called?

STEVE: Ghaniffs.

Then there was the big Hollywood party where, as the daughter of the family came into the room, a guest said, "Ah here comes the *pièce de résistance.*"

"I know the girl," Steve whispered. "Piece, yes. Resistance, no."

GROUCHO MARX: One time when Ike Eisenhower was campaigning for the presidency in New York he was speaking in a Jewish neighborhood and someone handed him a blintz. He had never seen one before and didn't know how to handle it, so he squeezed it too tight and it squirted all over his vest. In one second he lost the whole East Side.

ALLEN: He lost the whole *vest* side, too.

Though Allen is a serious student of the Vietnam dilemma, and has lectured on the subject, he has even joked about such grave subject matter.

"In 1955," he said, "Diem stamped out the sects. In 1961 Madame Nhu tried to stamp out sex."

At a benefit performance for Synanon, the self-help project that rehabilitates narcotics addicts, Allen said, "Ladies and gentlemen, by your presence here this evening you have certainly given this organization a great shot in the arm."

Riding together from Kennedy Airport in New York toward Manhattan one afternoon comedian Allan Sherman and Steve got to discussing places to stay.

"What's the name of that new hotel on the West Side?" Sherman said. "It's a kind of an austere place."

"The Waldorf-Austeria?" Steve hazarded.

Allen was being shown an apartment in New York.

Upon being told that it had two bathrooms, he said, "Well, two heads are better than one."

"A lot of people are advocating the end of the electoral college. I see no reason to go to that extreme. Probably all the electoral college needs is a good football team."

One night Allen was invited to address an audience at U.C.L.A. He got lost in what appeared to be the world's largest parking lot when he arrived on campus at 8 P.M. and then had considerable difficulty finding the Humanities Building, where he was scheduled to appear. Eventually he arrived late and in apologizing for his lateness said, "While wandering around outside in the lonely darkness I could not help being struck by the fact that it was strange that I should have been looking for the Humanities Building, for never have I seen an area so devoid of humanity."

Because it runs counter to his nature, Steve rarely uses sarcasm as a weapon in his humor. When he does, though, he employs it to devastating effect.

At a party, Allen and his wife were discussing a friend who seemed to be intoxicated.

"Tom isn't much of a drinker as far as I know," Jayne said. "He only likes to sip an occasional scotch and soda with friends."

"He must have a lot of friends," Steve observed.

A friend once said to Allen, "Do you think women's brains are as good as men's?"

"Absolutely," Steve responded. "Why they don't *use* them, I have no idea."

The producers of the motion picture *Tea and Sympathy* were not allowed to end the picture in the same way the

253

play concludes because the production code requires that sin must be punished. So the whole movie was done as a flashback. At the finish, actor John Kerr reads a letter that balances the moral books. Somebody asked Allen what the ending of the picture was. "It's very touching," he said. "The hero sits in the garden and reads a lengthy letter from the Johnston Office."

George Cukor, the famed director, was telling Allen about a 20th Century-Fox executive. "Peter Levathes is a most likeable chap," he said. "Skouras brought him to Fox some time ago and he's done an excellent job."

"Yes," said Walter Bernstein of the Fox staff, "he's a very bright man, too. As a matter of fact he used to teach languages."

"To Skouras, I presume," Allen said.

One night, on his TV show, Steve deftly placed a bunch of grapes into the mouth of a large elephant.

"What did that feel like?" asked announcer Johnny Jacobs.

"Like reaching into a suitcase full of wet liver," Allen said.

Pat Harrington, Jr., likes to tell of the time Allen was ad-libbing on his show with a certain Billboard Girl. Replying to Steve's question, "What are you doing professionally, miss?" the luscious young blond answered that she was making a film with Dean Martin, Peter Lawford, Sammy Davis, Jr., and Frank Sinatra.

Without the loss of a single beat and in perfect character, Steve said, "I hope you finish the picture alive."

On a trip to India with his family Allen was feted and

informed by Nawab Jung, of an Indian royal house. "In my country," said the Nawab, "weddings sometimes last fourteen days."

"In my country," Allen responded, "*marriages* sometimes last that long."

Alan King saw Steve and his wife walking slowly on East Fifty-fifth Street in the rain. They entered the Little Club, and Allen explained that he and his wife always enjoy walking in the rain in New York. "But in a dinner jacket?" King asked.

"Of course," Allen replied. "You never know when you're going to run into Leonard Lyons."

Hollywood night owls still quote the following TV exchange between Steve and Oscar Levant.

OSCAR: How come you felt qualified to write a book like *The Funny Men*, writing about a man like Eddie Cantor, for example, when you never saw him on Broadway and don't know him intimately?

STEVE: Oscar, is that a sound literary principle, that you have to personally know the men you write about?

OSCAR: Yes, I think so.

STEVE: Then I guess Jim Bishop is out of business.*

At a press conference in Hollywood, Allen was asked whether he considered himself a writer or a comedian. He replied, "I guess it goes something like this. When I write, I'm a writer. When I try to be funny, I'm a comedian. When I mow the lawn, I'm a lawn mower."

Steve wrote to thank the *Variety* critic who reviewed his TV show the Sunday it was on opposite a popular

* Bishop is the author of *The Day Christ Died* and *The Day Lincoln Was Shot*.

Crosby-Sinatra special and said, "More people may have read your review than saw the program."

Nature having given him the appearance of a not particularly aggressive home-appliances salesman, Allen seems to acquire physical distinctiveness only when he wears his horn-rimmed glasses. One day, on the way down to the Hudson Theatre on West Forty-fourth Street, where his program originated, Allen stepped out of a cab and offered the driver a bill. "Are you Robert Q. Lewis?" the driver asked.

"No," said Allen regretfully, "I'm Dave Garroway. We look a great deal alike."

Once, asked by an audience member whether he really had to wear glasses, Steve replied, "Yes. In fact, I'm the only person I know who has to wear contact lenses to see his glasses."

Allen does own contact lenses but seldom wears them. Once when he walked into the living room without his glasses, Jayne asked, "Are you wearing your contact lenses?"

"Yes," said Steve.

"I really can't see them," Jayne commented.

"I'm wearing them in my ears," said Steve.

Governor Sam Goddard of Arizona adopted as his political symbol the roadrunner, the small desert bird common to the southwest. Speaking at a dinner for the governor in Tucson, Steve said, "As a city boy from Chicago there was a time I was so ignorant as to what a roadrunner might be that I thought it was a fast streetwalker."

A Covedale, Ohio, couple, both oculists, watching Allen on television, decided that his glasses were sitting crookedly on his nose. They wrote a letter informing him of this observation, and offering to personally fit him with a proper pair the next time he visited nearby Cincinnati. Steve wrote back, "My glasses are on straight. It's my head that's crooked."

Now and then Steve will indulge in a brand of comedy that is in the classic Bob Hope stand-up monologue tradition.

In 1960 he spoke at a dinner in Denver, Colorado. "I'm staying at the Brown Palace Hotel," he said. "It's a truly beautiful place. I can see why the word "palace" is in its title. For several hours, however, since I'm not intimately familiar with Denver, I couldn't figure out why the word "brown" was involved.

"Until I filled the bathtub with hot water.

"I've seen coffee that was weaker than that stuff! It was a really weird experience. The water was cleaner after I got out of it!

"I wish I could say the same for myself!"

Allen is a master of the anticlimactic form of humor, as the following examples indicate:

In doing a takeoff of a TV quiz show, Steve once shouted, "And now, do you know what you have won? Look at the prizes on this card! A 1958 Cadillac, a Westinghouse Washer-Dryer, a complete Tiffany silver service, and a Revere movie camera. That's right, *you have won this card!*"

Allen's mother, the veteran vaudevillian Belle Montrose, began her career as a circus performer. Steve explained to some friends one evening that she worked without a net.

"What did she do?" someone asked.

"Sold popcorn," was the immediate answer.

A few of Steve's most amusing remarks have been unclassifiable except as pure uninhibited nonsense.

A girl on the secretarial staff tripped on the edge of a rug one day—for the second time in one season—and sprawled prone on the floor of Steve's office.

"I must be accident prone," she muttered as she got to her feet.

"I don't think so," Steve said. "I think you're prone-prone."

Don MacNeill recalls the following ad-lib exchange when Steve was a guest on his popular morning radio program *Breakfast Club*.

MacNEILL: Steve, how many stations is your program seen on now?

ALLEN: Forty-five stations, Don. Not all of them are TV stations, of course. Three of them are gas stations. But I'm sorry I was a little late getting into the studio.

MacNEILL: What happened?

ALLEN: Well, I stopped in the washroom to wash my hands and then I went over to the blower machine to dry them and discovered that the machine ran for an awfully long time. I stuck around for a while because I didn't want to waste all that hot air.

Opening night, at a party for the cast of *Mr. Wonderful*, Sammy Davis, Jr.'s Broadway show, the stars were depressed by the early reviews. Finally a call came through that Robert Coleman (he of the Rudolph Valentino hair style) had given the musical a better review than expected.

"What did he say?" somebody demanded.

"He gave the show two sideburns," Steve answered.

Barbara Siegel, who runs Barbara's Bookstore in Chicago, was doing a crossword puzzle. She asked Steve, temporarily in town, what a nine-letter word was for a completed football pass.

"Is it across or down?" asked Steve.

"Down."

"Oh, that's too bad. I only have the word for across."

He is also the leading (perhaps the only) practitioner of a peculiar form of humor that involves nothing more than starting a sentence one way and finishing it up another, with no planning having gone into the switch. He used to talk like this, he claims, as a child and is now unable to break the habit.

"When I saw the ugly cobra slithering toward me I drew back in panicky haste, for I knew that its slightest touch meant instant coffee." Most people don't laugh at material of that sort, so Allen has rarely bothered to expose his television audiences to it.

Although he is interested—in fact, active—in politics, Allen does not specialize, like Mort Sahl, in political jokes. One of his lines, however, has been borrowed by countless comedians:

"Remember, folks, go to the polls tomorrow and vote No on Proposition Yes!"

A friend told Steve that he had read about a man who jumped out of an airplane with no parachute and took one on the way down from another man who had jumped out of the plane at the same time.

"And," said Allen, "I'll bet the other fellow put up a hell of a fight for it, too."

Some of the men in his production office were talking to Allen about all the books that have been written about the *Titanic*, the "unsinkable" ocean liner that went down after a collision with an iceberg.

"There have been seven books about the *Titanic*," Steve said, "but I'd like to know why nobody's ever written a book about that iceberg? Why were seven-eighths of it hidden under water? There might have been a polar bear on that berg. Was he asleep at the icicle? These are the questions I'd like to see answered!"

Steve's attorney once asked him, "Do you have an account at the Irving Trust Company?"

"No," Allen said.

"Why not?"

"I don't trust Irving."

Doris Braverman Benson, who for several years was Allen's secretary, contributes the following recollection:

In the course of a conversation one evening with a prominent actor, the actor said that some years ago when he broke his foot his doctor gave him dope to kill the pain. He said he didn't know exactly what it was but he thought it was heroin or cocaine and was describing for us the wild elation he felt. However, he hastened to add, it was the only time he'd ever had it.

"And a good thing, too," Steve said. "With your foot like that you couldn't very well have kicked the habit."

In the days when crosscountry planes still had sleeper berths, a stewardess asked, "Mr. Allen, what kind of a call would you like in the morning?"

"A loud one," was the answer.

As the above examples illustrate, Steve's plays on words through the years have been numerous and varied, but those who have followed his witticisms find it hard to top a simple one-liner with which he let loose in an extemporaneous chat several years ago:

"What this country needs," he said, "is a good Françoise Sagan."

TV producer Bill Harbach, a close friend of Allen's, looked up one day from a paper he was reading. "What is statutory rape?" he asked.

"Raping a statue," was Allen's immediate answer.

On a highway north of Los Angeles, Allen and a companion passed a sign that said "Timber School."

"I know a fellow who went there," Steve said. "He majored in sawdust."

At a swank Hollywood dinner party the napkins were black linen. Somebody asked Allen why the napkins were black.

"I don't know," he said. "Perhaps the chef is in mourning."

EPILOGUE

The dissemination of humor in all its forms through the immensely powerful medium of television has withered in the early '60s, but the evidence is mounting that it may bloom again. By the summer of 1967 Allen, after two and a half years as master-of-ceremonies on *I've Got a Secret*, was on the CBS air with a weekly program reminiscent of his previous early-evening comedy hour. Jerry Lewis had his own show again. The Smothers Brothers, whose situation comedy show had lost out in the ratings handicap a couple of seasons earlier, were back with a more suitable and capacious comedy format. Joey Bishop had his own nightly forum. The resurgence indicated that comedy was suddenly "in" again. It would be redundant to add that never was it more urgently needed.